AF600510

THE CATHOLIC UNIVERSITY OF AMERICA
CANON LAW STUDIES
No. 110

OATHS IN ECCLESIASTICAL COURTS

AN HISTORICAL SYNOPSIS AND COMMENTARY

A DISSERTATION

Submitted to the Faculty of Canon Law of the Catholic University of America in Partial Fulfillment of the Requirements for the Degree of

DOCTOR OF CANON LAW

BY

EUGENE JAMES MORIARTY, J.C.L.
Priest of the Archdiocese of St. Paul

THE CATHOLIC UNIVERSITY OF AMERICA
WASHINGTON, D. C.
1937

Nihil Obstat:

VALENTINUS T. SCHAAF, O.F.M., J.C.D.,

Censor Deputatus.

Washingtonii, D. C., die 11 Maii, 1937.

Imprimatur:

JOANNES GREGORIUS MURRAY, D.D.,

Archiepiscopus Sancti Pauli.

Sancti Pauli, die 14 Maii, 1937.

Printed by

THE PAULIST PRESS

New York, N. Y.

TO THE MEMORY

OF

MY MOTHER

TABLE OF CONTENTS

FOREWORD

THE manifestation of truth to serve the impartial administration of justice is the purpose of every court of law. The integrity of courts is maintained as long as they make every effort to discover the truth of the controversy which has been submitted for adjudication. Among the means which the courts use to preserve their integrity and to secure justice is the oath which has been adopted into practically every known system of law from the crudest to the most perfected.

Undoubtedly, the intrinsic value of the oath arises from its deeply religious character and significance. The oath is an acknowledgment by man of God's infinite truth, knowledge and justice. It is an attempt to take man's judgment out of the sphere of the natural and the temporal and to place it in the realm of the supernatural and the eternal. He who takes the oath assumes a most serious responsibility. He places his testimony in the hands of God Himself, Whose all-comprehensive knowledge will discern and Whose unfailing justice will punish, in time or in eternity, any deliberate falsehood which shall pass his lips.

The purpose of this thesis is to discuss the important rôle which the Church assigns to the oath in her adjudication of trials. Extra-judicial oaths, such as those which are taken by cardinals, bishops, officials of the Curia, ecclesiastical judges, diocesan consultors and members of the Council of Administration upon promotion to office and those which are taken by clerics at the time of their incardination into another diocese, etc., do not fall within the ambit of this dissertation. For the sake of clarity it may be stated here that the probatory or judicial oath of Canon Law shall be considered under two main classifications: (a) Those which *corroborate* other proofs, and (b) those which constitute a special and independent means of proof of themselves.

The dissertation has been divided into two parts: An historical synopsis and a commentary. In the historical synopsis an attempt will be made to show that the Roman concept of the oath, crystallized in the Code of Justinian, embodied the suppletory, decisory, and estimatory oaths of the Code of Canon Law (Canons 1829-1836). A consideration of the early Germanic law will reveal the fact that two important canonical institutions arose from that system of law:

canonical purgation which was abolished in the eighteen century and the testimony of the seventh hand which still possesses probative force in processes to establish the impediment of impotence or the non-consummation of marriage, and in cases concerning the nullity of sacred ordination. Both systems of law gave rise to the oath of the parties to speak the truth. The gradual evolution of the oath of calumny into the oath of the parties to speak the truth shall be noted. Stress shall be laid on the particular Council of Rome held in the year 1725, which abolished the odious practice of tendering the oath to the defendant in criminal trials. The genesis of the oaths of having spoken the truth and of secrecy shall be traced to several important instructions of the Roman Congregations which appeared during the nineteenth century.

The last three chapters of the dissertation are devoted to a commentary on the present day canonical legislation pertaining to the oath in ecclesiastical trials. The order of the canons of the Code is followed as far as possible. In the chapter on the oath to speak the truth an attempt has been made to indicate the ceremonial that should surround the administration of the oath. The possibility of the parties' or the witnesses' refusal to swear is considered, as well as the value which may be placed on unsworn testimony. The penalties for falsehood and perjury are indicated. In the chapter, "The Oaths of Having Spoken the Truth, of Secrecy, and of Office," are discussed those trials which demand the administration of the oath of having spoken the truth; the conditions under which the oaths of temporary or perpetual secrecy must be imposed; and the obligations that fall upon the experts in taking the oath of office. The chapter entitled, "The Probatory Oath," treats of the suppletory, estimatory and decisory oaths, and the conditions required for their use.

The writer wishes to take this occasion to express the profoundest gratitude to the Most Rev. John Gregory Murray, S.T.D., Archbishop of St. Paul, for the opportunity of advanced study which his promotion of clerical scholarship has afforded. He also wishes to acknowledge his deepest appreciation of the invaluable assistance and suggestions given him by the Faculty of the School of Canon Law. He likewise wishes to thank the librarians of the University Library for the many courtesies they extended to him.

CHAPTER I

GENERAL NOTIONS OF THE OATH

Article 1. Definition of the Oath

Nominal Definition

The Latin language employs three words to designate an oath: (1) *jusjurandum*, (2) *juramentum*, (3) *sacramentum*. The words *jusjurandum* and *juramentum* are derived from the word *jus*, a right or a law. *Jusjurandum* is a combination of *jus* and the gerundive form of the verb *jurare*, the literal meaning being "a right or a law to be sworn."

The term *sacramentum* is derived from *sacrum*, a holy thing. It is certain that in Justinian's time (529-565) *sacramentum* was used in the general sense of an oath; [1] but in an earlier period of Roman legal history it had a far different connotation. In the period of the Legis Actiones (753 B. C.-*circa* 150 B. C.) it designated a wager or a pledge which, in certain instances, the loser in a trial forfeited to the priests.[2]

No doubt the fact that the priests who were *personae sacrae* obtained the wager was the reason why it was designated by the term *sacramentum*. Schmalzgrueber gives the canonical connotation of *sacramentum*. A *sacramentum* is an oath which is taken upon some sacred object, such as the book of the Gospels, altars or relics of the saints.[3]

Real Definition

An oath is an invocation of the Divine Name to witness an assertion or promise.[4]

[1] Codex (4.1) 11, 12.
[2] Leage, *Roman Private Law*, pp. 388-390.
[3] *Jus Ecclesiasticum*, Lib. II, Tit. XXIV, n. 1.
[4] Wernz, *Jus Decretalium*, V, n. 638; Canon 1316.

An oath is an *invocation* and in this it differs from a *vow;* the essence of a vow consists in a *promise* made to God.[5] An oath is an *invocation* of the *Divine Name.* Hence it follows that an invocation of creatures *as creatures* to witness an assertion or promise is not, strictly speaking, an oath; to raise an invocation of creatures to the dignity of an oath it is necessary to invoke them *in so far as the Creator is reflected in them, e. g.,* the heavens, the books of the Gospels, altars, etc. Furthermore, an invocation taken in the name of false gods cannot be properly classified as an oath. The purpose of an oath is that he to whom the oath is given may be infallibly assured of the truth of the assertion or the sincerity of the promise made. Such infallible assurance can only be obtained from an oath to the true God Who as the Supreme Truth, can neither deceive nor be deceived.[6]

Article 2. Requisites of An Oath

The requirements for the licit taking of an oath were laid down by the prophet Jeremias to the Jews of old: "And thou shalt swear: As the Lord liveth, in truth, and in judgment and in justice. . . . [7]

The Code of Canon Law has in Canon 1316, reiterated these three conditions of the prophet Jeremias: "Jusjurandum . . . praestari nequit nisi in veritate, in judicio et in justitia." *Truth* demands that the oath-taker testify to the truth, which he knows and as he knows it. In an assertory oath the sworn statements must be in harmony with the truth; in a promissory oath the oath-taker must have a *sincere* intention to fulfill the promise made. *Judgment* requires careful consideration of the reason for the taking of the oath. Some cause of real necessity or of great utility alone justifies the use of an oath. The requisite of judgment can be expressed negatively in the words of the Decalogue: "Thou shalt not take the name of the Lord, thy God, in vain." [8] *Justice.* (1) In the case of an assertory oath the affirmation or negation which the oath-taker wishes to corroborate must be lawful; (2) in the case of a promissory oath justice requires

[5] Schmalzgrueber, *Jus Ecclesiasticum,* Lib. II, Tit. XXIV, n. 3.

[6] Schmalzgrueber, *Jus Ecclesiasticum,* Lib. II, Tit. XXIV, n. 2.

[7] Jer. iv. 2.

[8] Exodus xx. 7.

that the oath-taker be able to assume licitly the obligation of fulfilling his promise.[9]

ARTICLE 3. DIVISIONS OF THE OATH

(A) *By reason of object* oaths may be divided into *Assertory* and *Promissory*. An *assertory oath* is one by which God is invoked to bear witness to the truth of an affirmation or denial of some fact present or past. A *promissory oath* is one by which God is invoked to attest to the sincerity of intention of the oath-taker with regard to a future act or omission of an act which he is now promising. The promissory oath always carries with it the notion of futurity.[10]

(B) *By reason of the place* where the oath is taken oaths may be *judicial* or *extra-judicial.*

A *judicial oath* is any sworn declaration taken in a judicial process; an *extra-judicial* oath is any type of oath not taken in a judicial process.[11]

Judicial oaths may be divided into:

I. *Those which pertain to the litigants and witnesses in a trial.*

II. *Those which pertain to the sentence of a trial.*[12]

I. *Oaths which pertain to the litigants and the witnesses.*

(a) *The Juramentum calumniae.* The full title of this particular oath is *juramentum calumniae vitandae, i. e.,* an oath to avoid calumny. Of great importance in Roman as well as in Canon Law, this oath was all but suppressed in the Code. It is mentioned but once in the new legislation—in Canon 2037, § 4, which imposes the taking of this oath on postulators and vice-postulators in causes of beatification. In the old law the *juramentum calumniae* was required of plaintiffs as well as of defendants in contentious cases. From the eighteenth century it became a well-established custom to exempt defendants in criminal trials from taking this oath. Five points were contained in the oath of calumny: (1) the litigant swore to his belief in the justice of his cause, (2) he swore that when in-

[9] Schmalzgrueber, *Jus Ecclesiasticum,* Lib. II, Tit. XXIV, n. 5; Reiffenstuel, *Jus Canonicum,* Lib. II, Tit. XXIV, n. 24.

[10] Vermeersch-Creusen, *Epitome,* II, n. 650, ad 2.

[11] Reiffenstuel, *Jus Canonicum,* Lib. II, Tit. XXIV, n. 10.

[12] Reiffenstuel, *Jus Canonicum,* Lib. II, Tit. XXIV, n. 11, 15.

terrogated he would not deny that which he believed to be the truth, (3) he swore that he would not knowingly employ false proofs, (4) he swore that he would not seek a fraudulent delay in the course of the trial, (5) he swore that he had not given and would not give, that he had not promised and would not promise anything save to those persons to whom the law permitted him to give or promise.[13]

(b) *The Juramentum malitiae.* Closely akin to the *juramentum calumniae* in the law of the Decretals was the *juramentum malitiae.* This oath has been entirely omitted in the new legislation. It was employed not to establish the truth in the whole trial as such, but to establish the truth in certain points of the trial. It could be demanded whenever there arose in the opinion of the judge a suspicion that one of the litigants had malicious intents in view. The oath of calumny was usually taken at the beginning of the trial after the *litis contestatio;* the *juramentum malitiae,* on the other hand, could be tendered either before or after the *litis contestatio,* in any part of the trial.[14]

(c) *The Juramentum de veritate dicenda.* This oath is promissory by nature. In taking it the oath-taker binds himself to tell the truth and nothing but the truth. The new Code enjoins the taking of this oath by the witnesses.[15] Furthermore, the parties themselves must take this oath whenever the public good is involved in a trial and whenever the judge deems its taking by the parties advisable.[16] However, this oath can never be tendered to a defendant in a criminal trial.[17]

(d) *The Juramentum de veritate dictorum.* This oath is assertory in character. By it the witness swears to the truth of the statements which he has made in the presence of the judge. As in the case of the *juramentum malitiae* of the Decretals, the tendering of this oath is left to the discretion of the judge.[18] It differs from the

[13] Glossa in c. 2, X, *de iuramento calumniae,* II, 7.

[14] Reiffenstuel, *Jus Canonicum,* Lib. II, Tit. XXIV, n. 17; Wernz, *Jus Decretalium,* V, n. 474.

[15] Canon 1767.

[16] Canon 1743.

[17] Canon 1744.

[18] Canon 1768.

juramentum de veritate dicenda in this that it is taken *after* the deposition has been made.

(e) *The Juramentum de secreto servando* is a promissory oath. By it the oath-taker promises that he will not make known to anyone the questions put to him and the answers given by him during the process.[19] The judge can impose this oath upon witnesses, experts, the parties and their advocates or procurators.

(f) *The Juramentum Septimae Manus* is a special oath taken in cases of impotency and in processes *super matrimonio rato et non consummato.* By it the fourteen character witnesses testify to their belief in the trustworthiness of the parties in the trial.[20]

II. *Oaths which pertain to the sentence of the trial.*

The Code treats of the oaths which pertain to the sentence of the trial in Canons 1829-1836, and classifies them under the heading, *De jurejurando partium.*

(a) The *suppletory* oath is one which the judge, after hearing the case, offers to one of the litigants when full proof is lacking. In taking the oath the litigant supplies the needed proof and is accorded the decision.[21]

(b) The *decisory* oath is one which one party, with the approval of the judge, tenders to his adversary in the trial under the condition that, if the second party takes it, he shall obtain the verdict without any further process.[22] The Code permits the decisory oath to be employed in deciding not only the principal cause, but incidental ones as well.[23]

(c) A *voluntary* oath is one which, by an agreement out of court, one party tenders the other under the condition that, if the second party takes the oath he will win the decision without any judicial proceedings.[24] This oath is also called the *juramentum conventionale.*

(d) The *estimatory* oath *(juramentum in litem)* can be de-

19 Canons 1769, 1623, § 3.

20 Canon 1975, § 1.

21 Reiffenstuel, *Jus Canonicum,* Lib. II, Tit. XXIV, n. 138. This oath was called the *juramentum necessarium* by pre-Code writers.

22 Reiffenstuel, *Jus Canonicum,* Lib. II, Tit. XXIV, n. 135.

23 Canon 1834, § 1.

24 Reiffenstuel, *Jus Canonicum,* Lib. II, Tit. XXIV, n. 133.

manded of a party who has suffered loss or damages in cases wherein the right to compensation has been established, but in which the amount of indemnity cannot be established with certainty. The judge may require the party who suffered damage to give a sworn estimate of the value of goods taken from or lost to him through the malice of the defendant.

Schmalzgrueber classified this oath under three categories:

(1) *Juramentum verae aestimationis,* by which the objective value of the goods lost or stolen was estimated.

(2) *Juramentum affectionis,* by which the subjective value attached to the goods by the owner was determined.

(3) *Juramentum super interesse singulari,* by which the *damnum emergens* and the *lucrum cessans* suffered by the plaintiff through the loss or destruction of his property were fixed.[25]

[25] Schmalzgrueber, *Jus Ecclesiasticum,* Lib. II, Tit. XXIV, n. 58.

CHAPTER II

THE ROMAN CONCEPT OF THE JUDICIAL OATH

ARTICLE 1. THE SUPPLETORY AND DECISORY OATHS IN JUSTINIAN LEGISLATION

ROMAN LAW used the phrase "the oath in a trial" *(jusjurandum in judicio)* to designate the suppletory oath and the term "necessary oath" *(jusjurandum necessarium)* to designate the decisory oath of Canon Law. Known and used extensively in earlier periods of Roman Law the two oaths were incorporated into the Code of Justinian who subjected them to certain modifications. It is to be noted especially that two very important innovations, bearing relation to the *jusjurandum necessarium* or the *jusjurandum in jure* found their way into the law of Justinian. In pre-Justinian legislation the *jusjurandum necessarium* could only be employed in certain limited cases. Now, the law permitted its use in *all* contentious cases. Formerly the plaintiff alone could make use of it, in the law of Justinian it could be tendered not only by the plaintiff to the defendant but by the defendant to the plaintiff as well.[1] It might be added that the *jusjurandum necessarium* no longer replaced the pronouncement of a sentence by the judge, for it now becomes merely a means of proof.

The new law of Justinian, in respect to suppletory and decisory oaths, comprised the following points: [2]

1. "If one of the parties tenders the oath to his adversary and, before his adversary takes it, recalls it, he shall not under any condition be permitted to have recourse to it a second time.

2. "If, however, one of the parties should tender the oath to the other party and then wish to revoke it, he shall be permitted to do so and to produce other evidence if he so desires. Recourse to other proofs is possible until the end of the trial.

3. "All oaths tendered by either the parties or the judge at

[1] Collinet-Gifford, *La Procedure par Libelle*, pp. 352-354.

[2] Codex (4.1) 11, 12.

the commencement, or in the course, or at the conclusion of the proceedings shall be taken by the opposing party in the presence of the judge without waiting for his final decision or the menace of an appeal.

4. "The party to whom the oath is tendered must take it or tender it back to his adversary.

5. "If the adversary, in turn, refuses to take the oath, the case is decided in favor of the party to whom the oath was originally tendered and appeal from the decision of the judge shall not be granted." To make these principles clear an example is necessary. Titus, in the trial, tenders the oath to Caius. Caius, instead of taking the oath, tenders the oath back to Titus. Titus, in turn, refuses to take the oath. In this event, by a fiction of the law, Caius wins the case and Titus is denied the benefit of an appeal.

6. The law permitted the party to whom the oath was tendered (a) to take the oath, (b) to tender it back to the offerer or (c) to refuse the oath. If the litigant chose the last of these three alternatives, the judge was empowered to decide the judicial effect of such a refusal. If the judge felt that the oath was rightfully tendered, he could decide against the party who thus refused to take the oath when tendered to him. However, it is important to note that the party had the right to appeal; the appellate judge would again consider the licitness of the demand of the oath and affirm or reverse the sentence accordingly.

7. The judicial oath described above could cover either the entire case or merely a certain point in the trial. If the oath centered about an incidental question before the court it would have the effect of an interlocutory sentence.

8. The tendering of the oath by one litigant to the other required the permission of the judge.

9. If the party, to whom the oath was tendered, was not present in court, the decision in regard to the taking, the tendering back, or the refusal of the oath could not be rendered by his attorney; the principal was granted a certain amount of time to appear in court. If the party lived in a province he could take, tender back or refuse the oath in the presence of a government official. The other litigant was permitted to be present if he so desired.

Article 2. The Oath of Calumny

Strictly speaking, the oath of calumny was not a probatory oath in Roman Law; nevertheless it assumed an all-important rôle in Justinian's time, because upon the taking or the refusing of it depended, in a large measure, the fundamental decision as to whether judicial proceedings should be permitted or quashed. The Law of the Decretals borrowed this oath from Roman Law and made it a *sine qua non* condition for all contentious cases.

This type of oath was known in the period of the early Roman procedure and given wide usage in the legislation of Justinian. It served a twofold purpose. On the one hand, it acted as a check to prevent any unjust and malicious prosecution of the defendant. On the other hand, it was intended to facilitate the administration of justice by furnishing the judge good grounds for believing that the defendant would not falsify evidence to obtain a favorable decision.

Under Justinian the *jusjurandum calumniae* became not merely one of the means but, the chief means, of avoiding vexatious litigation. The Digest of Justinian viewed "calumny" under two aspects: for the plaintiff it consisted in the prosecution of any defendant by vexatious and unjust litigation; for the defendant it consisted in any fraudulent delay of the trial.[3] To avoid both types of calumny Justinian incorporated the following principles into his Code.[4]

1. In all trials the litigants were compelled to take the oath of calumny.[5]

2. Advocates of the parties as well as the litigants themselves had to take the oath.[6]

3. The plaintiff swore that he sued the defendant not out of any motives of calumny but because he had a well founded belief in the justice of his suit.

4. The defendant swore that, in his estimation, he had a reasonable right to defend himself against the charges made by the plaintiff.

[3] Dig. (50.16) 233.

[4] Code (2.58).

[5] Code (2.58) 1.

[6] Code (2.58) 2.

5. To avoid the danger of collusion, judges could never dispense with the oath.[7]

6. If the plaintiff refused the oath, he lost the case as a dishonest litigant; if the defendant refused it, he would be considered as confessing all the charges set forth by the plaintiff.[8]

7. The oath was taken at the very beginning of the trial.[9]

Article 3. The Estimatory Oath

The *Jusjurandum in Litem.* Another oath which took its origin from Roman Law is the so-called *jusjurandum in litem.* Unlike the *jusjurandum calumniae* which was all but abolished in the Code of Canon Law, this oath is still retained and possesses probative force.[10]

In many cases the Roman judge had power to command a defendant to perform an action in accordance with the plaintiff's demand. If the defendant through malicious intent or culpable negligence[11] failed to obey the judicial order, his duty of performance became transformed into a duty to pay a pecuniary fine. To determine the amount of this fine the judge could call upon the plaintiff to make a sworn statement of the *damnum emergens* which resulted from such contumacious conduct on the part of the defendant.[12] The judge was not obliged to employ this oath or to fix damages in accordance with the sworn estimate of the plaintiff.[13] Furthermore he could limit the amount sworn to by the plaintiff.[14]

The Roman Law permitted this oath to be used likewise in cases where goods unjustly taken could not be returned because of their destruction.[15]

[7] Codex (2.58) 2.4.

[8] Codex (2.58) 2.5.7.

[9] Codex (2.58) 2.9.

[10] Canons 1832, 1833.

[11] Dig. (12.3) 2.

[12] Code (5.53) 2.4; Dig. (12.3) 2.

[13] Dig. (12.3) 4.2; Dig. (12.3) 5.1; Code (5.53) 1, 4.5.

[14] Dig. (12.3) 5.

[15] Code (8.4) 9.

ARTICLE 4. THE *Jusjurandum De Veritate Dicenda*

The *jusjurandum de veritate dicenda* is unique in that it found a common origin in both the Roman and Germanic law systems. In Roman Law, the *jusjurandum calumniae* corresponded to the *jusjurandum de veritate dicenda* of the parties in present canonical procedure. The *jusjurandum de veritate dicenda* was imposed upon all witnesses before giving their testimony. This law, enacted by Constantine, was incorporated by Justinian into his Code.[16]

ARTICLE 5. CLERICAL EXEMPTIONS FROM THE OATH

A striking concession to the Christian clerics and an eloquent testimony of the honor and esteem in which those of the clerical life were held by the Christian emperors appear in an enactment of the Emperor Marcian which appeared in the year 456. In harmony with ancient traditions of the Church the law forbids the taking or the tendering of the oath by clerics.[17] This enactment was destined to become of great importance in subsequent canonical procedure. The Emperor St. Henry II (1002-1025) referred to this law and thought that the oath to which it bore reference was the *jusjurandum calumniae* and that the law was enacted solely for the local clergy of Constantinople. To remove all difficulties St. Henry gave it universal application. He decreed that no bishop, abbot, cleric of any order, monk or nun should be compelled to take the *jusjurandum calumniae* but could delegate the oath to some trustworthy agent.[18]

[16] Codex (4.20) 9.

[17] Code (1.3) 25. 1b.

[18] *Leges Langobardorum, Liber Papiensis Henrici II*, 1—*M.G.H.*, *Leges*, IV, 584.

CHAPTER III

THE OATH OF PURGATION

About the time that Justinian and his jurists were framing and collecting the laws of the immortal *Corpus Juris Civilis,* events were taking place in the western part of the Roman Empire which were destined to leave a lasting impression upon the culture, the civilization and the laws of European nations. Forced by an inadequate amount of territory for cultivation in the home lands, Teutonic tribes, long checked in their advances by the might of the Roman military power, succeeded in crossing the frontiers of the Roman Empire on the Rhine and the Danube and in settling within the pale of the Roman frontier. Before their advance the Western Empire staggered, yielded and crumbled. From the fateful year 376 when the first invasion occurred to the year 800, when Charlemagne was crowned as the first Emperor of the Holy Roman Empire of the West, a process of fusion and transformation between the old and the new inhabitants of the old Roman Empire went on. The Franks in Gaul, the Anglo-Saxons in England, the Visigoths in Spain, the Lombards in Italy—all these Teutonic tribes intermarried with the native population, adopting many of the laws of the old regime and retaining others of their own. The Roman inhabitants became Teutonized and the newcomers became Romanized.

The Germanic form of trial procedure was destined to carry great influence in the civil and canon law of a later period. While, no doubt, differing greatly in detail the same fundamental concepts of the public administration of justice in court could be found among all the Teutonic races. Now to understand thoroughly the Germanic system of law, two facts of paramount importance must be borne in mind. In the first place the ancient German had a firm, deeply religious belief in a personal God, Who had an all comprehensive knowledge of mundane affairs. Being a God of infinite justice He would protect the innocent when wrongfully accused and, if necessary, would work a miracle to preserve him from any unjust punishment. On the other hand, the guilty could never escape His avenging hand. Resort to any subterfuge though he may, the criminal would always find that God would lay bare his crimes even in this life.

The second feature that must be remembered to enable one to interpret the German trial correctly is this: the German law system goes hand in hand with the German tribal organization. The Roman Law, in the later days at least, was territorial in application; that is, it bound all those who lived within its boundaries. In contrast, the German law emphasized the person rather than the place in its application. The law of the tribe bound all its members irrespective of any territorial considerations. Stress was laid upon the blood relationship existing between the members of the clan. In adjudicating disputes arising among individuals the judge would naturally turn to relatives or near neighbors of the litigants to verify the honesty and the integrity of the contending parties.

Article 1. The Germanic Trial of Compurgation

The preliminary stage of the German trial consisted in the appearance of accused and accuser before the court. The plaintiff, in the presence of the judge, made his accusation against the defendant, sometimes with others to support him. After the plaintiff made his plea the judge gave the defendant an opportunity to refute the charges raised by the plaintiff. After the plaintiff and the defendant had thus stated their charge and defense the judge determined which of the litigants should be the "proving party." The "proving party" was the litigant on whom the burden fell, not only of establishing the truth of his own allegations, but of disproving the charge or the defense of the opposing party. In the vast majority of trials the defendant was chosen as the "proving party."

Two means of proof could be employed. The "proving party" could call upon witnesses to swear to the truth of facts which they themselves had seen or heard. Often they were examined and gave their testimony separately.[1]

The second form of proof was the one by far more commonly

[1] *Leges Langobardorum, Liber Papiensis Karoli Magni*, 66—*M.G.H.*, *Leges*, IV, 500.

used. Here the "proving party" took an oath, affirming the truth of his statements, and at the same time several of his relatives or kinsmen took an auxiliary oath and swore that the oath of the principal was "clean" and "unperjured." These auxiliary oath-takers were known by the terms *eideshelfer*, "oath-helpers," *consacramentales, conjuratores*. They were not obliged to make known to the judge the reasons which motivated their belief in the veracity of the "proving party." In many cases the "proving party" was allowed to choose some of the oath-takers, his adversary choosing the others.[2] The number of the auxiliary oath-takers required for the process varied with the tribe and the question in dispute. In accusations of murder, for example, the number required by the defending party to purge himself varied from six to seventy-two.[3] The oath-takers were referred to frequently by the term "hand." Thus, the testimony of seven oath-takers was termed the testimony of the "seventh hand." The connotation of the word is obscure; Van Espen,[4] believing that the hand is a symbol of faith, implies that the oath-takers, by raising their hands in the act of swearing, signified their faith or their belief in the litigant by whom they were called into court.

It is important to note the essential difference between the oath of the witnesses, strictly so-called, and the oath of the *consacramentales* or the oath-takers. The witnesses swore to facts, alleged by the proving party and pertinent to the adjudication of the case. The oath-takers swore directly to their belief in the good character of the litigant. In modern day legal parlance they would be termed "character witnesses." The witnesses took their oaths independently of the litigant, the oath-taker swore with the litigant.[5]

If the charges, made by his adversary, were completely rebutted by the proving party and his witnesses or *consacramentales*, the judge was bound to consider the proof complete and award him a favorable verdict.[6]

[2] *Leges Langobardorum, Liber Rotharii*, 359—*M.G.H.*, *Leges*, IV, 385.

[3] *Lex Ribuaria*, XVII, 2—*M.G.H.*, *Leges* V, 218; *Lex Ribuaria*, XI, 2—*M.G.H.*, *Leges* V, 216.

[4] *Jus Ecclesiasticum Universum*, Pars III, Tit. 8, Cap. IV, n. 47.

[5] *The Continental Legal History Series*, VII, Engelmann-Millar, *A History of Continental Civil Procedure*, p. 159.

[6] Eichmann, *Das Prozessrecht des Codex Juris Canonici*, p. 19.

Article 2. Purgation and the Ordeal

The process of compurgation was based on the conviction in the Teutonic mind that God would inevitably wreak vengeance—even of an earthly nature—upon one who committed perjury. The ordeals arose from a conviction—equally firm—that no one truly innocent could be permitted by the Almighty to be adjudged guilty by his fellow men.

Ordeals were frequently resorted to (a) when suspicion of perjury arose in the process of compurgation, (b) when the proving party was unable to procure a sufficient number of compurgators, (c) when the defendant was a "rightless" person, barred by the law of the tribe from the privilege of compurgation.[7]

Throughout the earlier Middle Ages the chief forms of the ordeal were (1) the ordeal by walking through fire; (2) the ordeal by hot iron, in which the accused either carried for a certain distance in his hands, or walked barefoot over, pieces of hot iron; (3) the ordeal by hot water in which the accused was required to plunge his bare hand into boiling water and bring forth a stone or other object from the bottom; (4) the ordeal by cold water, in which the accused was thrown, bound hand and foot, into a pond or stream to sink if he were innocent, to float if he were guilty; (5) the ordeal of the Cross in which the accuser and the accused stood with arms outstretched in the form of a cross until one of them weakened; (6) the judicial combat in which the accused and the accuser or their representatives fought until one was slain, the victor being considered the innocent party.

Article 3. The Church and Compurgation

From the time that the Germanic tribes were converted to Christianity, the Church always distinguished between the so-called *compurgatio vulgaris* and the *compurgatio canonica*. By the *compurgatio vulgaris* the canonists of the Middle Ages designated that form of compurgation which, when it was necessary, resorted to the use of ordeals in one of its various forms. *Compurgatio canonica*

[7] *The Continental Legal Series*, VII, *A History of Continental Civil Procedure*, 154, 155.

on the other hand, consisted merely in the taking of the oath by the litigant and his oath-takers with no possibility of an impending resort to an ordeal.

In repeated pronouncements the Church roundly condemned the *compurgatio vulgaris* as a *tentatio Dei*. Such an unqualified disapproval can be seen in a decretal of Pope Stephen V. This Pontiff was requested to decide whether the ordeal by the hot iron or by boiling water should be imposed on a man and wife, whose child had died under mysterious circumstances, to prove themselves innocent of the charge of murder. In his reply Stephen calls such ordeals a *superstitiosa adinventio*. Under no condition can they be employed to test the innocence of the parties. It is for earthly potentates to pass judgment only on those crimes established by a free confession or proved by witnesses. The occult and the unknown must be left to Him Who alone knows the hearts of the children of men.[8] That great light of the Papacy of the ninth century, Nicholas I, sternly rejected the use of ordeals in the marriage trial of King Lothair and his queen, Teutberga, declaring that the duel constituted an infringement of both the laws of God and of the Church.[9] His Frankish contemporary, Agobard, metropolitan of Lyons wrote two books in condemnation of ordeals.[10] It is true that, to a certain extent, some prominent men of the period encouraged the practice of ordeals. Archbishop Hincmar of Rheims in his work *De divortio Lotharii regis et Teutbergae reginae*[11] advocated the use of the ordeal of cold water. Charlemagne thought the licitness of the ordeal to be beyond the question of a doubt.[12] But such cases must be considered exceptions; the ordeals finally yielded before the continued resistance of ecclesiastical authorities. The Fourth Council of the Lateran (1215) forbade any priestly approbation or blessing to be conferred on those who subjected themselves to the ordeal by hot or cold water or by the hot iron.[13]

[8] C. 20, C. II, q. 5.

[9] *Epist. ad Carolum Calvum*, *MPL*, CXIX, 1144.

[10] *Liber adversus legem Grundobaldi, Liber contra judicium Dei*—*MPL*, CIV, 125, 254.

[11] *MPL*, CXXV, 668, 669.

[12] *M.G.H.*, *Capitularia*, I, 150.

[13] Concilium IV Lateran, c. 18—Mansi, 22, 1007.

ARTICLE 4. *Purgatio Canonica*

While the Church so consistently set her face against the use of the *purgatio vulgaris,* she made wide use of the *purgatio canonica.* This mode of proof was employed frequently in criminal trials of the clergy. One must note carefully that it always remained a *supplementary* means of proof. It was resorted to when criminal charges remained unproven; and it was employed not so much to ascertain the truth or falsity of the criminal charges as to vindicate the good name of the cleric in the eyes of his fellow clerics and the laity.

Furthermore, the process of compurgation furnished the groundwork for the adjudication of processes *super matrimonio rato et non consummato,* and as such is preserved in the Code.[14]

The use of canonical purgation in ecclesiastical law covers a long span of years. Compurgation became common in Church courts during the years that elapsed between the reign of Charlemagne (814) and the Decree of Gratian (circa 1150). It was certainly known as late as Van Espen's time (1646-1728) who urged judges to employ it with extreme caution.[15]

Before Gratian's day, satisfaction by compurgation depended, apparently, not so much on the will of the judge as on the will of the accused. The purgation of Pope St. Leo III (816) furnishes a case in point. This pontiff, when accused of certain trumped-up charges, took an oath to prove his innocence and employed twelve bishops as oath-takers. In relating the story of his purgation Leo makes it perfectly clear that no coercion, no compulsion, obliged him to swear to his innocence in this manner. He wishes it to be understood that his action should not set a precedent for others. Like himself, the accused should feel at liberty to undergo the rite of compurgation or to refuse it if he sees fit.[16]

But, as time went on, compurgation ceased to be a work of supererogation which the accused could impose upon himself and became an obligation enforceable by judicial mandate. Gratian

[14] Canon 1975.

[15] *Jus Ecclesiasticum Universum,* Pars III, Tit. VIII, Cap. IV, n. 58.

[16] C. 18, C. II, q. 5.

laid down a general rule that clerics could be compelled by their lawful superiors to purge themselves of any accusations.[17]

Whatever latitude was accorded the defendant to refuse the process of compurgation definitely disappears in the Decretals of Gregory IX (1234). Alexander III (1159-1181) in answer to a query of the bishop of Genoa, declared that a bishop could compel a priest to take the oath of compurgation provided that the crime of which he was accused was of a public nature and accusers and witnesses were lacking. Nevertheless, to such a priest, Alexander gave the right of an appeal to a higher court which could render a decision as to whether or not the oath had to be taken.[18]

Innocent II (1130-1143) formulated the procedure to be used in the trial of a bishop accused of simony. Apparently the prosecution of the case had broken down badly. No definite charges could be proved against the accused bishop and witnesses were lacking. The Pontiff, therefore, decreed that the bishop could purge himself with the aid of bishops or abbots who could act as compurgators. However, different types of oath had to be taken by the defendant and the compurgators. The oath of the accused bishop had to be a *jusjurandum de veritate dicenda* denying the accusation; the compurgators had to take a *jusjurandum de credulitate*—that is an oath by which they swore to their belief in the truth of the defendant's statements.[19]

Nuns, accused of serious charges, could be forced to take the oath of purgation if the charges remained unproven.[20]

Innocent III (1198-1216) rigorously insisted on the need of purgation by those accused of criminal offenses. In reply to a letter of the Archbishop of Sens he commanded that a dean, charged

[17] *Dictum Gratiani ad c. 18, C. II, q. 5.* Gratian attempts to build up his point by quoting a letter supposedly written by Leo III to Charlemagne. C. 19, C. II, q. 5. This epistle commands bishops to impose the process of compurgation on priests who have been accused of crime. This canon was certainly not from the pen of Leo III as Gratian believed. The evidence that this canon was the work of Charlemagne himself, a firm believer in compurgation, is conclusive. Berardi, *Gratiani Canones,* Pars II, Tom. II, p. 203.

[18] C. 6, X, *de purgatione canonica,* V, 34.

[19] C. 5, X, *de purgatione canonica,* V, 34.

[20] C. 4, X, *de purgatione canonica,* V, 34.

with the delict of heresy, should be suspended from office and benefice until he purged himself with fourteen oath-takers who were to be chosen from the priestly order. When compurgation took place the Archbishop could restore the dean to his office and benefice. If the dean did not properly purge himself, he should remain deprived of his offices and should be sent to a monastery.[21]

The same Pontiff, Innocent III, was asked whether canonical purgation was necessary in the case of a bishop, of excellent reputation, who had been accused of certain crimes. The charges were highly improbable, in the estimation of fellow bishops, and well-founded suspicions of malice were lodged against the accusers. Innocent III ruled that in such a case necessity, of itself, did not call for compurgation; but if the procurator of the opposing party insisted on the point, purgation should be made by the bishop with two other bishops and three abbots acting as his oath-takers.[22]

Considering a case which was apparently the exact antithesis, Innocent III decreed that the privilege of purgation should not be extended to one against whom a grave crime had been definitely proven. Furthermore, an ordinary could not impose the rite of compurgation upon an *infamatus* pending an appeal.[23]

The fulminations of earlier Pontiffs decrying the use of the *purgatio vulgaris* are found reëchoed in the *Corpus Juris Canonici.* In the time of Lucius III certain authorities subjected a priest accused of homicide to the ordeal by cold water. Evidently, the accused survived the test, for the Pope was asked whether the priest had thus sufficiently cleared himself. Lucius replied that the *purgatio vulgaris* was not a recognized proof. If witnesses did not appear against him the priest should purge himself in a canonical fashion with five or seven other priests acting as *consacramentales.*[24]

A. *The Oath of the Compurgators*

With but one exception the compurgators mentioned in the title *De Purgatione Canonica* of the *Corpus Juris Canonici* took an oath

[21] C. 10, X, *de purgatione canonica,* V, 34.
[22] C. 12, X, *de purgatione canonica,* V, 34.
[23] C. 14, X, *de purgatione canonica,* V, 34.
[24] C. 8, X, *de purgatione canonica,* V, 34.

testifying to the good character of the accused or to their belief in his cause. Lucius III furnishes the exception. He declared that the compurgators could swear, either (a) that the accused took a "good" oath *or* (b) that the accused was innocent of the crime—*a crimine sit immunis*.[25]

B. Qualities of the Compurgators

The compurgators had to be men of honor, of good reputation, influenced neither by motives of love, nor of hate, nor of financial gain. Personal knowledge of the life and character of the accused was a prime requisite.

Those thus qualified could not be hindered by the judge or anyone else from taking upon themselves the rôle of compurgator,[26] nor should malevolence or ill-will be shown towards them. Judges should carefully investigate the character of the compurgators but should avoid excessive scrupulosity. Lucius III ironically reminded an over-zealous bishop that compurgators need not measure up to the same strict qualifications that were expected of candidates for ordination.[27]

The number of compurgators required for the trial varied; no definite rule was laid down in the decretals. Peers of the accused had to be chosen as compurgators. Laymen purged laymen, priests purged priests, bishops and abbots purged bishops.

Article 5. The Testimony of the Seventh Hand

A consideration of canonical purgation brings one to the origin of that form of witness proof known as the witness of the seventh hand. Gratian mentions the testimony of the seventh hand in his Decree[28] and assigns its origin to Gregory the Great (590-604). Berardi denies this Roman origin and traces its source to the Frankish capitularies, particularly to a capitulary in the reign of King Dagobert in the year 650.[29]

[25] C. 9, X, *de purgatione canonica*, V, 34.
[26] C. 7, X, *de purgatione canonica*, V, 34.
[27] C. 9, X, *de purgatione canonica*, V, 34.
[28] C. 2, C. 33, q. 1.
[29] Berardi, *Gratiani Canones*, Pars II, Tom. II, p. 23.

Although the mode of proof by the witnesses of the seventh hand possesses the general characteristics of every other type of canonical purgation one important difference must be noted. In the *purgatio canonica* but one party had to call in compurgators to testify to his probity of life; on the other hand *both* parties had to secure compurgators as character witnesses in trials in which the testimony of the seventh hand obtained.

The three matrimony cases of which the Decree of Gratian and the Decretals of Gregory IX took cognizance and in which the testimony of the seventh hand was commanded were cases of impotency. The Decree specifically commands the principals and the compurgators to lay their hands on relics while taking the oath. Rufinus points out that the principals took an oath to the *fact* of non-consummation while the compurgator swore to their *belief* in the non-consummation of the marriage.[30]

Celestine III and Honorius III followed the broad outlines of the impotency trial as laid down in the Decree. Celestine stated that relatives should be preferred as witnesses but if they be lacking, neighbors of good reputation could be admitted. If the impotency of one party was established the other party was free to enter a second marriage; but if the impotent party contracted a second marriage, perjury was presumed in the latter event and the judge could inflict a proportionate penance.[31]

Did this law intend to hold the witnesses of the seventh hand guilty of perjury if the impotent party thus entered a second marriage? A literal interpretation of the canon would render them subject to the crime. *"Verum si ille (i.e., pars impotens) aliam duxerit tunc hi qui juraverant rei perjurii teneantur . . ."* The *glossa,* however, with an eye to equity draws a needed distinction. If the witnesses of the seventh hand swore in good faith they were judged innocent of the sin of perjury; bad faith rendered them guilty and penances could be imposed upon them as well as upon the principals.[32]

[30] *Summa,* p. 434.

[31] C. 5, X, *de frigidis et maleficiatis et impotentia coeundi,* IV, 15.

[32] Glossa in c. 5, X, *de frigidis et maleficiatis et impotentia coeundi,* IV, 15, ad verba *hi qui.*

Honorius III added the sworn testimony of midwives concerning the virginity of the woman to the testimony of the seventh hand. Furthermore, he omitted the clause of Celestine III which commanded the parties to return to their previous status should the impotent party attempt a second marriage.[33]

[33] C. 7, X, *de frigidis et maleficiatis et impotentia coeundi,* IV, 15.

CHAPTER IV

THE JUDICIAL OATH IN THE *CORPUS JURIS CANONICI*

ARTICLE 1. THE OATH OF WITNESSES

THE oath usually demanded of witnesses in canonical trials was the *jusjurandum de veritate dicenda.* In some instances, as shall be shown, the Germanic system of compurgation led some Pontiffs to substitute the *jusjurandum de credulitate* for the *jusjurandum de veritate.*

Gratian in the second part of his Decree laid down a few general rules for the taking of the oath. Judges must not permit perjurers to swear at trials.[1] Later canonists, however, placed limitations upon this unqualified rule of Gratian. The glossators distinguished between those oaths which conferred a privilege and those which imposed a burden upon the oath-taker. In the latter species of the oath they included the *jusjurandum calumniae* of the parties. Such an oath must be taken by perjurers, lest they should appear to gain an advantage from their depravity.[2]

The Decree of Gratian forbade those under fourteen years of age to swear.[3] For the taking of oaths it was deemed seemly that people should be fasting.[4] Oaths should not be taken from Septuagesima Sunday to the octave of Easter; nor from the first Sunday of Advent to the octave of the Epiphany, nor on Sundays, Ember Days or days of the major litanies.[5]

Referring more specifically to the oaths of the witnesses Gratian reaffirmed the law of Justinian[6] which required witnesses to give

[1] C. 14, C. XXII, q. 5.

[2] Glossa in c. 14, C. 22, q. 5, v. *causa.*

[3] C. 15, C. XXII, q. 5.

[4] C. 16, C. XXII, q. 5.

[5] C. 17, C. XXII, q. 5.

[6] Codex (4.20) 9.

their testimony under oath.[7] One taking such an oath must testify to facts which come within the scope of his personal knowledge or to facts apprehended through the corporal senses.[8]

The Decree mentions a negative as well as a positive mode for taking the oath to tell the truth. Leo IV, writing to the bishops of Brittany, required the witnesses in a criminal trial to take an oath on the four Gospels that they would speak no falsehood.[9] Pelagius I, on the other hand, required witnesses to take a positive oath *to speak the truth.*[10]

The obligation of taking the oath before testifying included clerics as well as laymen, but clerics when acting as witnesses in the trials of laymen were forbidden to take the oath in the presence of a layman.[11]

These general requirements for the *jusjurandum de veritate dicenda* of the witnesses became more clearly defined in the Decretals of Gregory IX. Honorius III stated that no testimony prejudicial to another's cause should be believed unless the one giving the testimony first takes the oath to tell the truth.[12] Innocent III considered the oath to be of such supreme importance that he refused to exempt religious, acting as witnesses, from taking the oath.[13] This refusal of Innocent was reaffirmed by Honorus III.[14]

Innocent III established an important concession for the remission of the oath of the witnesses. This pontiff permitted witnesses to testify unsworn, if the opposing litigant gave his consent to such an omission of the oath.[15] This principle was with modifications incorporated into the Code.[16]

The law of the decretals required judges to demand the oath from the witnesses, not only in trials of first instance, but in appellate cases

[7] C. 3, C. IV, q. 3.
[8] C. 15, 20, C. III, q. 9.
[9] C. 3, C. II, q. 4.
[10] C. 20, C. III, q. 9.
[11] *Dicta Gratiani* ad C. 22, C. XXII, q. 5.
[12] C. 51, X, *de testibus et attestationibus*, II, 20.
[13] C. 39, X, *de testibus et attestationibus*, II, 20.
[14] C. 51, X, *de testibus et attestationibus*, II, 20.
[15] C. 39, *de testibus et attestationibus*, II, 20.
[16] Canon 1767, § 3.

as well. A previous taking of the oath offered no grounds for exemption.[17]

The law, likewise, determined the allegations to which witnesses had to testify when they were brought in for the sake of establishing feasible exceptions as recognized by the court. A witness testifying to a dilatory exception could not be forced to give testimony and swear to the main issue in the case, but a witness to a peremptory exception could be thus coerced.[18]

Witnesses in a marriage trial involving consanguinity took two oaths. They first swore that they would give their testimony, uninfluenced by any motives of hate, friendship or financial gain. After that the witnesses swore that the facts pertinent to the case were handed down by their ancestors as the truth,[19] and that they themselves believed in the truth of their statements. One should note that this oath was a *jusjurandum de credulitate* rather than a strict *jusjurandum de veritate dicenda.* The Fourth Council of Lateran reaffirmed this law of Blessed Eugene III, but added this condition: *"Sed nec tales [testes] sufficiant nisi jurati deponant se vidisse personas [majores]."* More direct evidence was thus insisted upon.[20]

Nicolaus de Tudeschis—known also under the name of *Panormitanus*—maintained the view that the oath *de veritate dicenda* of the witnesses included an implicit oath *de secreto servando.*[21] This secrecy, the canonist held, the witnesses were obliged to observe until the publication of the evidence. Other canonists espoused his opinion, among them Pirhing [22] and Reiffenstuel.[23] An explicit mention, however, of the oath *de secreto servando* in Canon Law cannot be found in the *Corpus Juris Canonici.*

ARTICLE 2. THE *Jusjurandum de Veritate non Dicenda*

In the twelfth and thirteenth centuries there arose a certain abuse whereby some defendants in criminal trials bound those who would be

[17] C. 17, X, *de testibus et attestationibus,* II, 20.

[18] C. 29, X, *de testibus et attestationibus,* II, 20.

[19] C. 5, X, *de testibus et attestationibus,* II, 20.

[20] C. 47, X, *de testibus et attestationibus,* II, 20; Mansi, 22, 1039-1042.

[21] Panormitanus in C. 17, X, *de testibus et attestationibus,* II, 20, n. 13.

[22] *Jus Canonicum,* Lib. II, Tit. XX, Sect. II, n. 116.

[23] *Jus Canonicum Universum,* Lib. II, Tit. XX, n. 470.

called in as witnesses to swear that they would not testify to any allegations harmful or detrimental to the defendants. Such an oath was known by the paradoxical term *jusjurandum de veritate non dicenda* and was tantamount to a promissory oath of perjury. This abuse met with the sternest condemnation and the most unqualified disapproval of the Roman Pontiffs. Writing to Alexander III, the Archbishop of Genoa had drawn the Pope's attention to the prior of a neighboring monastery who, when accused of simony and adultery, bound certain witnesses by oath not to testify against him. In answer to this bold effrontery of the prior, Alexander declared that such an oath was devoid of all binding force and commanded that the witnesses be forced to appear and testify to the *truth.*[24]

Innocent III had to contend with even more glaring abuses of this kind in high places. A certain Archbishop Alferius was threatened with arraignment in ecclesiastical court to answer criminal charges leveled against him. Thereupon the Archbishop's kinsmen took matters into their own hands by browbeating some of the witnesses out of appearing at the trial, and by imposing upon others an oath *de veritate non dicenda.* Innocent was convinced that drastic action was needed to curb such acts of villainy and injustice. Accordingly he decreed a ban of excommunication against those who would hinder in any way the admission of witnesses to the trial. Witnesses upon whom had been imposed the iniquitous oath *de veritate non dicenda* were released from any supposed obligation arising from it, and Innocent made it clear that, if the relatives of the Archbishop would in any way hinder the witnesses from appearing in court, the Archbishop himself must be suspended from office because it was to be presumed that the crimes had been committed with at least his tacit consent.[25]

An important legal principle can be validly drawn from these two examples: the obligation of a witness to tell the truth was so sacred in the eyes of the canonists that it superseded all other sworn obligations of loyalty and obedience to one's superior.

[24] C. 4, X, *de testibus cogendis,* II, 21.

[25] C. 45, X, *de testibus et attestationibus,* II, 20.

Article 3. Perjury

Several passages in the *Corpus Juris Canonici* show that the hand of canonical justice fell heavily upon those found guilty of perjury. The Decree of Gratian imposed a forty days fast of bread and water upon a perjurer. Following the fast the perjurer had to perform heavy penances for seven years, and after that period of time he had to perform lighter penances in expiation of his sin until the day of his death.[26]

The same note of severity can be seen in a law of Celestine III, who decreed that a cleric, either of major or minor orders, legitimately convicted of perjury, must be deposed by an ecclesiastical judge. If the cleric remained obstinate he must be excommunicated and anathematized. If these drastic punishments failed to correct him he must then be handed over to the secular arm for the punishments of the state.[27] No less severe was another decretal of the same period which commanded that a subdeacon who brought false charges against a higher cleric should be deposed, publicly scourged and cast into exile.[28] Privation of benefice was another penalty inflicted upon a perjured cleric.[29]

Some examples show, however, that the law tempered justice with mercy in the punishment of perjurers. Thus Innocent III inflicted the comparatively mild penalty of suspension *ab ordinandi potestate* upon a perjured bishop. It might be noted that this was a medicinal rather than a vindictive punishment, for Innocent remarked that the bishop should remain suspended until he merited forgiveness.[30] Gregory IX pursued a similar policy of leniency in stating that, if fitting penances had been performed, an occult sin of perjury did not prohibit the exercise of clerical orders or promotion to higher orders.[31]

Apparently no ecclesiastical censures were pronounced against perjured laymen yet penances could be imposed upon them. Perjurers were forbidden to testify in court.[32]

[26] C. 18, C. VI, q. 1.
[27] C. 10, X, *de judiciis*, II, 1.
[28] C. 1, X, *de calumniatoribus*, V, 2.
[29] C. 10, X, *de jurejurando*, II, 24.
[30] C. 15, X, *de temporibus ordinationum et qualitate ordinandorum*, I, 11.
[31] C. 17, X, *de temporibus ordinationum et qualitate ordinandorum*, I, 11.
[32] C. 54, X, *de testibus et attestationibus*, II, 20.

Article 4. The Oath of Calumny

The oath of calumny played the same all-important rôle in the Decretals that it did in the Code of Justinian. The plaintiff who refused to take the oath lost his right of action, as a dishonest litigant. Refusal of this oath by the defendant was tantamount to a confession and admission of the charges set forth by the plaintiff.[33]

In the twelfth century the laws of Justinian and Emperor St. Henry II which forbade clerics to take the *jusjurandum calumniae* were subjected to certain modifications. Honorius II permitted bishops and clerics to take this oath, if they had received permission to do so from their superiors (*i. e.*, Pope or bishop).[34] This restriction was abolished by Lucius II, who commanded all clerics to take the *jusjurandum calumniae* when acting as litigants. No contrary custom could be maintained against this new legislation.[35]

A doubt arose as to whether the oath of calumny should be taken by the principal or his representative. Writing on this question Pope Blessed Eugene III (1145-1153) warned ecclesiastical judges against an indiscriminate tendering of the oath to the attorney in lieu of the principal. The nature of the trial and the character of the litigants must determine the point whether the judges should tender the oath to the parties or their procurators.[36] The decretals permitted bishops to delegate their representatives in court to take the oath; but if they themselves chose to swear, they did so [*manibus*] *propositis sed non tactis Evangeliis*.[37]

A. The Jusjurandum Calumniae and the Jusjurandum de Veritate Dicenda of the Parties

It is impossible to determine when it became customary to demand of the parties the oath *de veritate dicenda* instead of the *jusjurandum calumniae*. Undoubtedly, a certain decretal of Honorius II (1124-1130) exerted some influence in bringing about the change.

[33] C. 7, X, *de juramento calumniae*, II, 7.
[34] C. 1, X, *de juramento calumniae*, II, 7.
[35] C. 5, X, *de juramento calumniae*, II, 7.
[36] C. 3, X, *de juramento calumniae*, II, 7.
[37] C. 7, X, *de juramento calumniae*, II, 7.

This Pontiff ordained that in *causae spirituales*, the oath of calumny was to be neither tendered nor received, for, he remarks, such trials are to be judged by the principles of canonical equity, not by the strict principles of law. The *glossa* to this passage states that in such trials it was customary to demand of the litigants the oath *de veritate dicenda.*[38]

Both oaths were mentioned by Boniface VIII in the *Liber Sextus*. He declared that if the two oaths were not taken at the very beginning of the trial they could be supplied at any point of the trial. An unintentional omission of the two oaths would not render the process null and void. Furthermore, Boniface advised the use of both oaths in all trials even in *causae spirituales.*[39] He extended this rule to appellate cases.

The same Pontiff permitted judges to exact from litigants a third oath called the *juramentum malitiae*. This oath could be demanded either before or after the *litis contestatio* and could be employed whenever the good faith of one or both the parties was called into question.[40]

B. The Abolition of the Oath of Calumny

One must trace the disappearance of the *jusjurandum calumniae* from ecclesiastical courts, not to any positive enactment forbidding it, but to a custom against the law. Schmalzgrueber (1663-1735) adverts to the non-use of the *jusjurandum calumniae* even in his day.[41] Wernz, a pre-Code author, proves the reasonableness of this custom in opposition to the law by the following argument:

The *juramentum calumniae* was introduced into ecclesiastical courts by human, not by natural or positive divine law; and a human law can be abrogated by a contrary custom which is reasonable and legitimately prescribed. That this particular custom was reasonable could be proved by the fact that if men are of good character this oath is not necessary. On the other hand, the greater the evil among men, the greater their likelihood of falling into the

[38] Glossa in c. 2, X, *de juramento calumniae*, II, 7, ad verba *rebus spiritualibus.*

[39] C. 1, *de juramento calumniae*, II, 4 in VI to.

[40] C. 2, *de juramento calumniae*, II, 4 in VI to.

[41] *Jus Ecclesiasticum*, Pars II, Tit. VII, n. 5.

sin of perjury. Hence, the fact that in the one event the oath would be superfluous and in the other supposition the oath would be a proximate occasion for the sin of perjury justifies the supposition that the development of a custom in opposition to the law was altogether reasonable.[42]

Article 5. The Suppletory and Decisory Oaths in the *Corpus Juris Canonici*

The revival of Roman Law in the twelfth and thirteenth centuries brought about in Canon Law a return to the Roman concept of proof presentation. Roman Law accepted as a cogent means of proof the decisory or suppletory oaths which were employed when documentary or attestive proof was lacking or deemed insufficient. Recognition was accorded these two types of probatory oaths by Canon Law as is evident from a number of the decretals.

Clement III permitted a clerical plaintiff in a damage suit against a layman to establish and prove his case by taking a suppletory oath. The cleric was unable to procure witnesses in his behalf; and Clement, while admitting that the testimony of one individual did not ordinarily constitute full proof in a trial, declared that the honor of the clerical state warranted this exception to the general rule.[43]

But the use of the suppletory and the decisory oaths was by no means restricted to clerics. At a usury trial the judge could in any part of the process demand of one of the parties an oath *de veritate dicenda* when other proofs were lacking.[44] Nicolaus de Tudeschis believed that the oath was suppletory rather than decisory in character.[45] The same author maintained that such an oath could be employed not only in usury trials but in *all* trials in which the question of sin was involved.[46]

While the oath found extensive use in the adjudication of trials, the canonists of the period, bearing in mind the great sanctity and

[42] *Jus Decretalium*, V, n. 479, p. 379.

[43] C. 5, X, *de testibus cogendis*, II, 21.

[44] C. 32, X, *de jurejurando*, II, 24.

[45] A suppletory oath was one which the *judge alone* could tender to one of the parties; a decisory oath was one which *one of the litigants* could tender to the other party with the permission of the judge.

[46] Panormitanus, Lib. II, Tit. XXIV, Cap. 31, nn. 1, 4b.

reverence of the oath, inveighed against its excessive and unnecessary use. Alexander III permitted the oath to be employed when other means of proof were lacking, but declared that a plaintiff who had fully proved his case should not be compelled to swear.[47]

Gregory IX laid down definite rules for the taking and tendering of the suppletory and necessary oaths. Reaffirming the Code of Justinian [48] he stated that a decisory oath tendered by a judge could not be refused without a good cause. But, if an oath was tendered by one litigant to another, it could either be refused or tendered in return. When the plaintiff had failed to prove his case the judge had no alternative but to discharge the defendant. On the other hand, if the presumption were in favor of the plaintiff, an oath could be tendered to the defendant to prove his innocence. (Here one finds a curious intermingling of the Germanic oath of purgation and the Roman decisory oath.) But if the judge, after taking into account the character of the litigants and the nature and circumstances of the trial would deem it better, he could offer the decisory oath to the plaintiff in lieu of the defendant.

To these rules Gregory states an exception in these words: "*Nec liceat convento famosa actione referre hujusmodi juramentum.*" [49] Unfortunately the words are ambiguous and admit two interpretations diametrically opposed one to the other. They could mean that in an *actio famosa* either (a) the defendant could not tender back the oath to the plaintiff, or (b) the plaintiff could not tender back the oath to the defendant. Nicolaus de Tudeschis seems to hold the first interpretation of the words. He believed that the defendant in an *actio famosa* must be presumed to have a better knowledge of the truth than the plaintiff and because of this should be compelled to take the oath.[50]

Van Espen embraces the second interpretation of the words when he uses this decretal to support his view that the oath should never be tendered to a defendant in a criminal trial or even in a contentious trial when infamy of law would fall upon the defendant by an un-

[47] C. 2, X, *de probationibus*, II, 19.

[48] Codex (4.1) 12.

[49] C. 36, X, *de jurejurando*, II, 24.

[50] Panormitanus, Lib. II, Tit. XXIV, C. 36, n. 12.

favorable decision.[51] Reiffenstuel likewise followed this view. Quoting Farinacius, he defined a *causa famosa* as one which inflicted infamy of fact and law and injured the litigant's reputation among good and respectable men. In such causes, Reiffenstuel maintained, the decisory and suppletory oath could not be employed.[52]

Durantis made the use of the suppletory oath depend on the type of the trial and the amount of evidence presented by the parties. If the case was *famosa* or *criminalis* the oath could not be employed because proofs in such cases must be clear and self-evident. Contentious cases Durantis divided into those which were of great importance (*magna et ardua*) or of small importance (*parva*). In a *causa magna et ardua*, Durantis advised extreme caution in the use of a probatory oath. It could never be employed in a *causa spiritualis*, *e. g.*, in a trial concerning the matrimonial bond.[53] He permitted greater latitude to judges in tendering a suppletory oath in a *causa parva*.

If the evidence presented by both parties was about equal Durantis favored the tendering of the oath to the defendant, but admitted the view of other canonists who believed that the judge should tender the oath to the plaintiff.[54]

Article 6. The Estimatory Oath in the *Corpus Juris Canonici*

This oath was incorporated into Canon Law by Gregory IX. In dealing with a damage suit he commanded the plaintiff to first establish, by competent witnesses, the fact that violence had been inflicted by the defendant. A probatory oath of the plaintiff was sufficient to prove the property had been lost through the misconduct of the defendant. The judge could then make an estimate of the value of the goods lost, demand an oath from the plaintiff that the estimate was a true one and condemn the defendant accordingly.[55]

[51] *Jus Ecclesiasticum Universum*, Pars III, Tit. VII, C. 8, *de juramento suppletorio ob defectum probationum*, nn. 19, 20.

[52] *Jus Canonicum*, Lib. II, Tit. XXIV, n. 217.

[53] *Cf.* Glossa in c. 34, X, *de jurejurando*, II, 24, verb. *absoluto:* "in tali casu non dico juramentum deferendum quantumque honesta sit persona quia hic agitur quasi de statu hominum."

[54] *Speculum Juris*, Lib. II, Partic. II, *de juramenti delatione*, nn. 5-10.

[55] C. 7, X, *de his quae vi metusve causa fiunt*, I, 40.

CHAPTER V

THE PROBATORY OATH AFTER THE *CORPUS JURIS CANONICI* TO THE NEW CODE

ARTICLE 1. THE PROVINCIAL COUNCIL OF ROME (1725)

A FAR-REACHING change in the use of the probatory oath was effected in a provincial council of Rome held in the year 1725 under the auspices of Pope Benedict XIII. This council brought about the complete suppression of the practice of tendering the oath to a defendant in a criminal trial.

> It must not be judged reprehensible that, because of the changing conditions of the times and for reasons of necessity and utility, human laws and customs sometimes vary . . . Because of this we consider the practice of the judges in some secular and ecclesiastical courts, of demanding the oath *de veritate dicenda* of defendants in criminal trials, to be well-established—even though said practice was never commanded by any law. On the other hand, as daily experience shows, no advantage accrues to the prosecution from this practice and nothing is proved against the defendants by this custom (as the defendants usually deny the crimes of which they are charged). So true is this that not only does no necessity of demanding the oath exist; nay more, the sacred character of the oath demands and requires the prohibiting of the oath under these circumstances. Hence it is that we, having weighed both sides of the question carefully and following as closely as possible the practice of well-recognized tribunals, command that all oaths tendered to defendants in criminal trials be completely abolished and suppressed. . . Nor do we wish an oath of this kind to be exacted of the defendants in the future (unless they are examined as witnesses in the trials of other individuals) by any judge or official under any pretext, cause or artifice; contrariwise an examination thus conducted and all the acts of the process shall be null and void and shall lack all binding force against the criminal.[1]

[1] Concilium Romae, Tit. XIII, Caput 2—Mansi, 34 B, 1872.

Several facts must be carefully borne in mind concerning this law of the Council. While it was a local enactment and embraced only the Italian dioceses it gained widespread recognition by the fact that it emanated from the very center of Christendom itself. It was a definite forerunner of Canon 1744 which clearly gave the principle of this particular law universal application. Furthermore, it sounded the death knell to the process of canonical purgation, for canonical purgation stood or fell on the power of the judge to demand an oath of the defendant in a criminal trial.

ARTICLE 2. THE OATHS *de Veritate Dicenda* AND *de Secreto Servando* IN MATRIMONIAL CAUSES

During the nineteenth century several important instructions appeared which contained rules for the use of the oath in matrimonial trials.

The Congregation of the Council in an instruction of the 22 August, 1840, required the petitioner in processes *super matrimonio rato et non consummato* to take an oath *de veritate dicenda* before giving testimony. After the testimony had been given, the petitioner had to take the oaths *de veritate dictorum* and *de secreto servando*. The oath *de secreto servando* consisted in a sworn promise to keep secret the questions proposed and the answers given until the publication of the process.[2]

An instruction of the Congregation for the Propagation of the Faith of the year 1883 demanded the oath *de veritate dicenda* of all who gave testimony in matrimonial cases. The witnesses swore singly. Before the witnesses took the oath the judges gave a fitting admonition concerning the sanctity of the oath, especially when the witnesses were illiterate and uneducated. The witnesses touched the book of the Gospels while taking the oath and repeated the oath before each deposition. The judge could impose the oath *de secreto servando* upon the witnesses, if in his estimation the nature of the case demanded it.[3]

[2] S. C. C., Instr., 22 Aug., 1840—*Fontes*, n. 4069.

[3] Instr. S. C. de Prop. Fide, 1883, n. 12—*Coll.*, n. 1587.

Article 3. The English Law

In the reign of King William IV (1830-1837) there was enacted an English statute which was destined to modify and effect Canon Law for a number of years. This law rendered it unlawful "for any justice of the peace or other person to administer, or cause or allow to be administered, or to receive, or cause or allow to be received any oath, affidavit, or solemn affirmation touching any matter or thing whereof such justice or other person hath not jurisdiction or cognizance by some statute in force at the time being." [4]

As the courts of the Catholic Church possessed no juridic standing in the English law, and her judges no recognition, the practical import of this statute was obvious. The Catholic ecclesiastical courts of England and Ireland could not, under penalty of the civil law, tender or receive any oath. When the first Provincial Council of Westminster was held in the year 1852 cognizance had to be taken of this difficulty. On the one hand, the English hierarchy realized the intrinsic value of a sworn deposition; on the other hand the hierarchy had been but recently reëstablished; opposition was rampant, and a violation of the civil law could well be calculated to bring on a fresh wave of religious bigotry. A compromise was necessary, and this compromise found expression in the rules for the criminal trials of clerics. In such a trial the oath could not be imposed upon witnesses; but the judge could ask them whether *they were prepared* to support their allegations by oath should the occasion arise.[5] If the witnesses answered in the affirmative, their statements would possess the same probative value as the oath itself.

Possibly because of a fear that a similar prohibition existed in the United States, the Congregation for the Propagation of the Faith in an instruction of July 20, 1878, forbade witnesses in criminal trials to take the oath. But if the witnesses did not refuse the oath and declared their readiness to confirm their statements by

[4] 5 and 6, William IV, c. 62 s. 13.

[5] Concilium Provinciale Westmonasteriense I, X, *Modus procedendi in consilio capiendo a concilio investigationis priusquam finaliter deiiciatur rector missionarius*, n. 10—Mansi, 44, 767.

oath the courts should make an annotation of this declaration in the acts.[6]

This absolute prohibition of the oath was modified a few years later. Instructions of the Congregation for the Propagation of the Faith in 1883 and of the Congregation for Bishops and Regulars on June 11, 1880, required the use of oaths in criminal trials, *if the civil law did not prohibit it.* The judge could demand of all witnesses in such a case the oaths *de veritate dicenda* and *de secreto servando.*[7]

The use of the oath in trials was definitely imposed on the Church in the United States by a decree of the year 1884. An instruction of that year permitted judges in matrimonial cases to demand of witnesses the oaths *de veritate dicenda* and *de secreto servando.* No reference is made to any possible prohibition of oaths by the civil law.[8]

CONCLUSION

This study of the history of canonical probatory oaths may be summarized in the following points. The suppletory, estimatory and decisory oaths have been adopted from Roman Law sources. The oath *de veritate dicenda* of the parties in contentious cases is an outgrowth of the Roman Law *jusjurandum calumniae* which, by force of custom, it gradually superseded. The oath *de veritate dicenda* of the witnesses originated in both the Roman and Germanic law systems. The oath of secrecy *(de secreto servando)* was implicitly contained in the oath *de veritate dicenda* of the law of the Decretals; explicit mention of this oath is found in the instructions of the Congregation of the Council (1840) and the Congregation for Bishops and Regulars (1883). The Congregation of the Council likewise prescribed the use of the oath *de veritate dictorum.*

[6] S. C. de Prop. Fide, 20 July, 1878, *de commissione investigationis*, n. 11—*Acta et Decreta Concilii Plenarii Baltimorensis III*, p. 295.

[7] Instr. S. C. de Prop. Fide, 1883, n. XVIII—*Coll.* 1586; Instr. S. C. Ep. et Reg., 11 Junii, 1880, n. 18—*Coll.* 1534; *Fontes*, n. 2005.

[8] *Instructio de judiciis ecclesiasticis circa causas matrimoniales*, Pars I, *De processu Matrimoniali*, n. 12—*Acta et Decreta Concilii Plenarii Baltimorensis III*, p. 264.

The Germanic system of compurgation formed the basis for the oath of the witnesses of the seventh hand in processes *super matrimonio rato et non consummato* and in impotence trials. Canonical compurgation gained extensive recognition in the Canonical courts of the Middle Ages but was finally suppressed by the Council of Rome (1725) which prohibited the tendering of the oath to the defendant in criminal trials.

CHAPTER VI

THE OATH TO SPEAK THE TRUTH

Obligations Arising From the Taking of the Oath

CANON 1767, § 1, clearly outlines the obligations which fall upon the person who takes the oath to tell the truth. By taking this oath the oath-taker promises to speak the complete truth in answer to all the questions asked of him while under oath. He must exclude all ambiguities [1] and all mental reservations in making answer to the interrogations put to him. The oath-taker not only binds himself to speak the complete truth; he is also bound to tell ***the exclusive truth ("... de ... sola veritate ...")*** in responding to the questions asked, as well. To express it negatively, he cannot without perjury inject any element of falsehood in his depositions.[2]

If the oath-taker is a witness he makes an implicit promise, by taking the oath, to give his testimony for the sake of truth and justice alone and uninfluenced by any motives of hatred, friendship, favor or financial gain. Hence he must speak the truth even if it be detrimental to the party in whose behalf he has been called upon to testify.[3]

Finally, it should be noted that the oath while obliging the oath-taker to speak the complete and exclusive truth in answer to the questions asked does not require him to impart any information which is not contained within the scope of the interrogations.[4]

ARTICLE 1. THE OATH OF THE PARTIES TO TELL THE TRUTH

It has been pointed out in the historical section of this dissertation that the law of the Decretals adopted from Roman Law the oath

[1] Blat, *Commentarium Textus Codicis Iuris Canonici,* IV, *De Processibus,* n. 274, p. 292.

[2] Reiffenstuel, *Ius Canonicum Universum,* Lib. II, Tit. XX, n. 466.

[3] Reiffenstuel, *Ius Canonicum,* Lib. II, Tit. XX, n. 466; Schmalzgrueber, *Ius Ecclesiasticum,* Lib. II, Tit. XX, n. 87.

[4] Reiffenstuel, *Ius Canonicum,* Lib. II, Tit. XX, nn. 465, 468.

of calumny—an oath by which the judge was assured of the good faith of the litigants in entering a trial. During the last few centuries a custom of omitting the oath of calumny in ecclesiastical trials arose and as a consequence this oath fell into desuetude. The Code, apparently, took cognizance of this custom against the law when it omitted in its processual law all previous canonical legislation which required the taking of the oath of calumny. Hence, since the Code takes no notice of this oath in the law of judicial procedure it may be considered, by virtue of Canon 6, 6°, to be definitely abolished.[5]

The oath of calumny was divided into several sections or points, one of which was equivalent to an oath of the parties to speak the truth. This oath has been preserved in the Code and finds expression in several canons of the fourth book.

A. Conditions Required for the Tendering of the Oath

Canon 1744 lays down the general conditions for the taking of the oath by the parties to tell the truth. The judge, the canon states, cannot tender the oath to the accused in a criminal trial; he should exact it of the litigants in contentious cases wherein the public good is involved; he can demand it of the litigants in other types of contentious trials whenever in his prudent judgment he deems it advisable to tender it.

This canon gives universal application to the decree of the Council of Rome (1725), which forbade the tendering of the oath to a defendant in a criminal trial. The great wisdom and justice inherent in this canonical enactment is easily apparent. It definitely removes a proximate occasion for the terrible sin of perjury. If the person accused is actually guilty of a crime he is no longer faced with the alternative of either suffering condemnation and disgrace through confession of his guilt or of saving his reputation by adding a sin of perjury to the sin of which he knows in his conscience that he is guilty. If he is condemned he knows that it is the testimony of another and not his own honesty which condemned him. If the accused is innocent of the charge leveled against him natural

[5] Noval, *De Processibus,* Pars I, n. 435; the oath of calumny is still used in canonization processes. *Cf.* Canon 2037, § 4.

equity demands that, when the charges are found to be devoid of all foundation, the accused should be absolved forthwith and not be required to furnish any new evidence of his innocence.

The question might easily arise whether the phrase *in causis criminalibus* of Canon 1744 should be given a strict or broad interpretation. In other words should the judge abstain from tendering the oath to an accused only in those trials which have for their object the declaration or infliction of penalties? [6] Or does the prohibition of the oath extend to those contentious cases in which the defendant would incur infamy if he lose the trial?

Commenting on the decree of the Council of Rome, Bouix [7] believed that the prohibition of the oath extended not only to defendants in criminal trials strictly so-called but to defendants in trials which were *famosae, arduae* and *notabiles* as well. The Code has not preserved these distinctions of pre-Code authors. It distinguishes merely between trials which are contentious or criminal. One can safely say that Bouix's opinion regarding the prohibition of the oath to a defendant in difficult *(arduae)* or notorious *(notabiles)* causes can no longer be accepted; for Canon 1744, far from interdicting the use of the oath in such trials, definitely prescribes it in trials which concern the public good, and such trials are frequently equivalent to the difficult and notorious processes of which the pre-Code authors speak. As for *causae famosae* (*i. e.,* contentious trials in which the defendant suffers infamy, loss of good repute, etc., upon condemnation) it must be admitted that the Code does not forbid the tendering of the oath to the defendant in trials of this nature. However, one must bear in mind the prescription of Canon 1743, § 1, which permits a litigant to refuse to admit a delict committed by himself. When such a circumstance arises the party may take exception to a question concerning a delict or may refuse to answer it or may even evade it, but he cannot, without perjury, tell a deliberate falsehood.[8]

The judge must demand the oath of the parties in contentious

[6] Canon 1552, § 2, 2°.

[7] *De Judiciis*, II, 200.

[8] A Coronata, *Institutiones Juris Canonici*, III, *De Processibus*, n. 1270, p. 175; Lega, *De Judiciis Ecclesiasticis*, n. 451, 7°.

cases involving the public good. The oath acts as a guarantee that justice will be impartially administered in a trial through the full revelation of the truth. The law binds the judge to take advantage of this important guarantee of the oath in trials involving the public good; for, while an erroneous adjudication of a private trial will inflict damage on one of the litigants alone, a faulty sentence in a trial pertaining to the public good will cause serious harm to the public welfare of the Church as a whole. Hence the parties must take the oath in all trials which concern ecclesiastical rule and discipline or the good of souls, in all trials pertaining to the matrimonial bond or concerning the nullity of sacred orders or pertaining to the obligations inherent in them, in all trials in which the defender of the bond or the promoter of justice must intervene (exception being made, of course, for the defendant in a criminal trial).[9] Although the oath should never be omitted in cases involving the public good it is not required for the validity of the process.[10]

In several instances the Code commands the judge to ascertain the truth in certain points of a trial (whether it pertains to the private good of the litigants or to the public good of the Church) by administering a special oath to one of the litigants. These instances are the following:

(a) A person who wishes to establish a dilatory exception after the joinder of issue must swear that he was not previously aware of the exception.[11]

(b) If a party wishes to reject a witness after the three days allotted by law to him for doing so, he must establish by oath that he was not previously aware of the witness's deficiencies.[12]

(c) If a party denies possession of a document which the judge wishes him to produce in court, he must support his denial by oath.[13]

Whenever he deems it advisable to do so the judge can exact the oath of the litigants in trials involving their private good. This procedure would be expedient, for example, if one of the parties

[9] Wernz-Vidal, *De Processibus*, n. 422, p. 364.

[10] A Coronata, *De Processibus*, n. 1271, p. 177.

[11] Canon 1628, § 1.

[12] Canon 1764, § 4.

[13] Canon 1824, § 3.

wished to make a judicial confession. To emphasize the importance and the juridic effects of his confession on the mind of the party the judge could require him to make his confession under oath.[14]

B. The Refusal of the Parties to Take the Oath

The law of the Decretals made the refusal of a party to take the oath equivalent to a tacit confession of guilt.[15] More logically and more in accordance with the principles of equity the Code permits the judge to estimate the importance of the litigant's refusal to swear and to decide whether it is equivalent to a confession or not.[16] When such cases arise the judge should determine to his own satisfaction the *cause* of the refusal to swear. In some instances it may not infrequently happen that a party, having a poor or unreliable memory, will have justifiable scruples over telling even unintentional falsehoods. To decide that his refusal to take an oath is equivalent to a confession would be, to say the least, rash and reckless judgment on the part of any judge. In other cases a litigant may show a definite attitude of contempt, haughtiness, stubbornness or of measured condescension towards the officials of the court. Obviously such an individual could be more easily suspected of entering trial in bad faith, and the judge could more reasonably construe his refusal to be a confession.

C. Mode of Procedure in Administering the Oath

The oath should be tendered to the parties before they are interrogated. Since interrogation of the parties can take place at any stage of the trial until the closing of the evidence[17] the oath can likewise be administered at any period of the process.[18] The oath may

[14] Noval, *De Processibus,* Pars I, n. 435, p. 303.

[15] C. 7, X, *de juramento calumniae,* II, 7.

[16] Canon 1743, § 2; Roberti, *De Processibus,* II, n. 320, p. 18.

[17] Canon 1742, § 3. Canon 1861 permits the judge to question the parties even after the closing of the evidence in causes which never become *res adjudicatae* (Canon 1903), and in cases where documents have been but recently found or where witnesses because of some legitimate impediment have been unable to appear before.

[18] Noval, *De Processibus,* Pars I, n. 435, p. 303.

cover the interrogations asked during the entire trial or it may embrace only those questions addressed to the litigant in a section of the trial.[19] The parties must always take the oath personally.[20] Lawful representatives may take the oath in behalf of incapacitated and moral persons.[21] A judge, auditor or delegate may proffer the oath. As a general rule the parties should swear in the hall of the tribunal. However, the Code grants an exemption from this rule to cardinals, bishops, and illustrious persons whom the civil law excuses from the obligation of appearing before a judge. These classes of persons may take the oath in any place of their own choice. Likewise all persons prevented from appearing in court by illness or for any other physical or moral cause or by reason of their state of life, such as cloistered nuns, may take the oath in their respective residences.[22]

The party when cited makes his appearance before the judge on the predetermined day and hour. The judge before administering the oath should never fail, under any condition, to give the admonition commanded by Canon 1622, § 2. It is difficult to overestimate the importance of this admonition for on its use or omission the great moral and religious force and the intrinsic proving value of the oath may frequently stand or fall. In his exhortation the judge should remind the oath-taker that he is about to invoke the all-holy God of power to witness and judge the truth of what he says; that, should deliberate falsehood fall from his lips, he is guilty of the awful sin of perjury; that perjury calls down upon him most severe punishments of the Church. If the trial involves the validity of a sacrament, such as marriage or holy orders, the judge should not hesitate to remind the oath-taker that any willful falsehood may render him guilty not only of perjury but of coöperation in a grave sin of sacrilege as well.

To further emphasize the importance of the oath and the seri-

[19] Roberti, *De Processibus*, II, n. 320, p. 19.

[20] Canon 1746: before the Code a procurator possessing a special mandate could swear in the name of the principal. *Cf. Regulae servandae in iudiciis apud S. R. Rotae Tribunal*, 4 Aug., 1910, n. 146, § 2, 142—*AAS*, II (1910), 827.

[21] Roberti, *De Processibus*, II, n. 320, p. 19.

[22] Canon 1770, § 2, 1°, 2°; A Coronata, *De Processibus*, n. 1271, footnote 9.

ous responsibility which its taking implies the judge should take pains to surround its tendering with a certain amount of impressive ceremonial. The taking of an oath before a large Crucifix and lighted candles will not fail to impress the fact on the party that the oath is a most sacred act of religion and not an empty, meaningless formula. The Code prescribes that a priest should swear with his hand over his heart, a layman with his hands touching the book of the Gospels.[23] It may not be amiss to remark here that the Bible or the book of the Gospels should be of a size sufficient to remind the oath-taker of the gravity of the act which he is about to perform. While the Code does not specify whether the book of the Gospels should be in the Latin tongue or in the vernacular it would appear preferable to use a vernacular edition, for the oath-taker then knows at a glance the nature and the character of the book upon which he swears.

The Code permits the oath to be administered in either the declaratory or interrogatory form. In the latter case the judge recites the formula and the oath-taker assents to it.[24] In the declaratory form the oath-taker repeats the formula, word for word, after the judge. While both forms are admissible, the declaratory form appears to be the more desirable from the viewpoint of psychology; for the deliberate, word for word repetition of the formula will frequently impress the grave importance of the oath upon the taker more than the short, matter of fact statement "I do."

Irrespective of the form he uses, however, the ecclesiastical judge will do well in avoiding the careless, slipshod, superficial and hasty procedure which often accompanies the administration of the oath in civil courts. To render the oath the respect it deserves and to foster proper reverence for it in the mind of the taker the judge should recite the formula slowly, distinctly and with a becoming grave tone of voice.

Since the deaf and dumb are not excluded from acting either as witnesses or litigants in an ecclesiastical trial it follows that they

[23] Canon 1622, § 1.

[24] As, for example: Judge: "Do you swear to tell the truth, the whole truth and nothing but the truth in reference to the facts about which you will be interrogated?" Oath-taker: "I do."

may be called upon to swear. To avoid all possible ambiguities and misunderstandings which might arise, the preferable method of administering the oath to them is to present them with a written copy of the oath and to have them sign it after reading it through. If a mute still possesses the faculty of hearing, the interrogatory formula of the oath may be employed; he could express his assent by a nod or any other affirmative sign.

The written report of the oath should indicate the year, month, day, hour and place wherein the oath is taken; it should mention, furthermore, the judge who tendered it, the promoter of justice and the defender of the bond, the notary and the party or procurators who were present at its taking; the trial to which the oath had reference; the name of the party and his rôle in the process (whether plaintiff or defendant); the admonition given by the judge; the formula sworn to; the signature of the party [25] and the signatures of the judge and notary. If the interrogations and the oath are combined, one set of signatures will suffice for both the testimonies and the oath. If the oath is refused, mention should be made of this fact, and the causes alleged for refusal.[26]

D. *Penalties for Falsehoods and Perjury*

A party, witness or expert who gives false testimony in an ecclesiastical trial should be punished by a temporary removal from legitimate ecclesiastical acts.[27] This penalty forbids the guilty person to administer ecclesiastical goods and property, to act as judge, auditor, referee (*relator*), defender of the bond, promoter of justice and of faith, notary, chancellor, messenger, bailiff, advocate and procurator in ecclesiastical causes; to act as sponsors in the sacraments of Baptism and Confirmation; to vote in ecclesiastical elections; and to exercise the right of patronage.[28]

If the falsifier has spoken the untruth while under oath he is

[25] If the party could not or would not sign the formula mention should be made of this fact.

[26] Roberti, *De Processibus,* II, n. 320, p. 19.

[27] Canons 1743, § 3; 1755, § 3; 1794.

[28] Canon 2256, 2°.

guilty of perjury and should be punished with a personal interdict if he is a layman, with suspension if he is a cleric.

These penalties are *ferendae sententiae* and may be inflicted by the judge in the trial or by the judge delegated to make the interrogations.[29] However, the judge should never punish a perjurer without first consulting the ordinary and obtaining his permission.[30] From the fact that the penalties mentioned in Canon 1743, § 3, are modified by the phrase *ad tempus* it may be assumed that the punishments inflicted on perjurers are vindicative in nature. They can be imposed for a certain definite length of time only. The interdict which is inflicted upon a perjured layman is *ab ingressu ecclesiae* [31] which forbids attendance at divine services and prohibits ecclesiastical burial. Nevertheless, if the interdicted person attends divine service in a church he need not be expelled; if he is buried in the Church ecclesiastical authorities are not obliged to exhume and remove the corpse.[32] An interdict *ab ingressu ecclesiae* does not prohibit assistance at divine services in oratories, whether public, semi-public or private; nor does it forbid the reception of the Sacraments.[33]

Clerics, inasmuch as they are bound to practice a higher degree of virtue than laics [34] become subject to the graver penalty of suspension when guilty of the crime of perjury. In itself the law embraces all those who have received first tonsure; [35] but the Roman Pontiff alone can inflict this sanction upon cardinals, Legates of the Apostolic See and bishops.[36] Furthermore, since clerics in minor orders have scarcely any active powers of order or of jurisdiction, the judge can inflict the penalty of interdict in lieu of suspension upon them when they are found guilty of perjury.[37]

As the word *suspensione* of Canon 1743, § 3, lacks any modify-

[29] A Coronata, *De Processibus*, n. 1270, p. 176.

[30] Haring, *Der Kirchliche Eheprozess*, p. 52.

[31] Canon 2291, 2°; Blat, *De Processibus*, n. 242, p. 262.

[32] Canon 2277.

[33] Conran, *The Interdict*, pp. 140-142.

[34] Canon 124.

[35] Canon 108, § 1.

[36] Canons 2227; 1557, § 1.

[37] Blat, *De Processibus*, n. 242, p. 262.

ing or restrictive phrase it would seem to follow that the suspension incurred by the crime of perjury implies a suspension of all power of orders as well as of jurisdiction.[38]

Canon 1743, § 3 permits the judge to use his own discretion in determining the length of time within which the perjured layman or cleric must remain under the ban of ecclesiastical penalties. The following consideration should be weighed in determining the duration of the penalties.

(1) The importance of the trial. Other factors being equal perjury in a trial involving the public good will frequently have greater evil effects than perjury in a trial concerned solely with the private welfare of the litigants.

(2) The influence which the perjured statements had or might have on the sentence of the trial. Suppose, for example, that the testimony of a qualified witness [39] carried such great weight that the trial was adjudicated in accordance with the facts made manifest by his testimony and later the testimony is found to be false. Naturally it can be presumed that the penalty inflicted on the perjurer will be greater than that imposed on a witness or party whose sworn declarations little affected the outcome of the trial.

(3) The notoriety of the perjury. Generally, the more notorious the evil deed, the greater the amount of scandal which it will cause. Hence a notorious act of perjury should be punished more severely than an occult one.

(4) The factors mentioned in Canons 2199-2213. Thus proper cognizance must be accorded to such attendant circumstances as ignorance, age, fear, etc., and they should be intimately borne in mind when administering penalties for perjury.

Article 2. The Oath of the Witnesses to Tell the Truth

Canon 1767, § 1 prescribes the general rule that witnesses before giving testimony must swear to speak the whole and entire truth. The term *testis* includes not only witnesses in the strict sense of the

[38] Canon 2279, § 1.

[39] Canon 1791, § 1.

term, but experts and witnesses of the seventh hand as well.[40] The formula of the oath tendered to witnesses of the seventh hand *in ratum non consummatum* matrimonial processes and in cases concerning the nullity of sacred ordination is the same as that tendered to all other witnesses. The difference between ordinary witnesses and witnesses of the seventh hand lies in the content of their depositions. The former testify to facts which they have seen or heard; the latter testify to the good character of the litigants.

By the oath the witness obliges himself to answer truthfully all the questions which may be put to him during the course of the trial. Its scope, then, extends to the entire process and can never be limited to certain points (as may be the oath of the parties).[41]

The question may arise whether, when a witness is called upon to testify at several sessions, he should take the oath at each deposition. One can admit that since the oath covers the entire trial a single administering of it will sufficiently fulfill the requisites of the law. On the other hand, the Code does not expressly forbid the judge to tender it more than once to the same witness; and undoubtedly a second tendering of the oath will have the important psychological effect of recalling to the mind of the witness the grave and important responsibility incumbent upon him to speak the truth.

The parties or their procurators should be informed of the time and place appointed for the tendering of the oath to the witnesses to give them an opportunity of being present if they so desire.[42] Canon 1763, however, permits a judge to dispense from this requirement whenever in his prudent judgment he deems it best to keep the names of the witnesses for one party unknown to the other litigant.[43] Even in this exceptional case each party has the right of attendance when his own witnesses take the oath.

[40] Canon 2145, § 2; *Regulae servandae in processibus super Matrimonio rato et non consummato*, nn. 40, 67; *Instructio servanda a tribunalibus dioecesanis in pertractandis causis de nullitate Matrimoniorum*, Normae, n. 96, § 1—*AAS*, XXVIII (1936), p. 333.

[41] A Coronata, *De Processibus*, III, n. 1295, p. 208.

[42] Canon 1767, § 2; Lega, *De Judiciis Ecclesiasticis*, n. 484, p. 425.

[43] This procedure would be expedient if the judge foresees that the witness will be subjected to a temptation of bribery or exposed to cruelties; Roberti, *De Processibus*, II, n. 339, p. 51.

Nevertheless, the presence of the parties is not required for the validity of the process and the parties can raise no plea of exception on the grounds of their voluntary or involuntary absence.[44] This opinion differs from that of pre-Code authors who permitted a party who was involuntarily absent from the taking of the oath by the witnesses to bring an exception against their examination.[45]

A. *The Omission of the Oath*

While the omission of the witnesses' oath does not affect the validity of the process [46] the judge should never fail to tender it to the witnesses unless a just cause intervenes.

The Code permits the judge to omit the tendering of the oath to the witnesses under two conditions: (a) if both parties in a private trial allow the witnesses to give testimony unsworn; [47] (b) if the witnesses are unsuitable or suspected.[48]

Equity demands that *both* parties in a private trial give their consent to the remission of the oaths of the witnesses, for the omission of the oath involves the rights of both parties and damage could fall upon either or both parties if, through the omission of the oath, false evidence is presented. Furthermore, the principle *quod omnes tangit, ab omnibus approbandum* [49] has application here. The parties must give their express consent to the remission of the oath; tacit consent will not suffice.[50] A judge cannot act contrary to the wishes of the parties and demand the oath of the witnesses when the parties in a private trial prefer to dispense with it.[51] By mutual con-

[44] Muniz, *Procedimientos Eclesiasticos*, III, n. 314, p. 248; Augustine, *A Commentary*, VII, p. 219.

[45] Reiffenstuel, *Ius Canonicum*, Lib. II, Tit. XX, n. 496.

[46] Muniz, *Procedimientos Eclesiasticos*, III, n. 314, p. 249.

[47] Canon 1767, § 3.

[48] Canons 1767, § 1; 1758, 1757, §§ 1 and 2.

[49] Reg. 29, R. J. in VI°.

[50] Schmalzgrueber, *Jus Ecclesiasticum*, Lib. II, Tit. XX, n. 90.

[51] Schmalzgrueber, *Jus Ecclesiasticum*, Lib. II, Tit. XX, n. 91.

sent the litigants may exempt all the witnesses from taking oath or merely a certain number. No dispensation from the oath should be granted to the witnesses in a trial involving a *restitutio in integrum* in behalf of minors.[52]

In trials involving the public welfare, such as matrimonial and criminal processes, the judge should not sanction the omission of the oath of the witnesses even when the parties desire it.[53] Nay more, in administrative criminal processes witnesses and experts must be excluded from testifying unless they first take the oath.[54]

Pre-Code writers approved the custom of permitting illustrious personages such as bishops and high civil magistrates to give their testimonies unsworn.[55] Nowhere in the Code can one find any recognition or approval of this custom; and, if one can form a conclusion from the following case, the Rota has definitely repudiated it. The priest claimed that he had been incardinated into a certain diocese. The bishop of the diocese denied this claim. As all documentary evidence was lacking, the priest called upon the former bishop of the diocese who had subsequently been raised to the dignity of an archbishop to testify that he had incardinated the priest into the diocese. The archbishop did so. Nevertheless, the case was decided against the priest, and one of the grounds on which the Rota rejected the testimony of the archbishop was that he had given his allegations without taking the oath.[56]

The second instance in which the judge may omit the tendering of the oath to the witness occurs whenever the latter is unfitted (*non idoneus*) or suspected. The Code, it should be noted, does not positively forbid the judge to administer the oath to unfitted or suspected witnesses, but strongly dissuades him from doing so.[57] The objection

[52] Noval, *De Processibus*, Pars I, n. 484, p. 338.

[53] *Instructio servanda a tribunalibus dioecesanis in pertractandis causis de nullitate matrimonorum*, Art. 96, 142—*AAS*, XXVIII (1936), 333, 336.

[54] Canon 2145, § 2.

[55] Schmalzgrueber, *Jus Ecclesiasticum*, Lib. II, Tit. XX, n. 89; Reiffenstuel, *Jus Canonicum*, Lib. II, Tit. XX, nn. 477-480.

[56] S. R. R., *Londonen. Incardinatio*, 9 Jan., 1912, Coram R. P. D. Antonio Perathoner, dec. II, n. 9—*Decisiones*, IV (1912), 19-22.

[57] "Non idonei et suspecti . . . generatim iniurati audiantur." Canon 1758.

cannot be urged that the value of their testimony is lessened through the omission of the oath, for Canon 1758 assigns only corroboratory and confirmatory value to their depositions.

Unfitted witnesses are those who have not reached the age of puberty, and the weak-minded.[58] Hence boys who have not attained the age of fourteen years and girls under twelve years of age must be classified as unsuitable witnesses.[59] Persons under the age of puberty are considered unfitted for testimony because of the danger that they will not sufficiently understand the gravity of the sin of perjury or that they could be easily bribed in view of their immatured character or inconstant dispositions.[60]

Those who are of unsound mind are likewise unsuitable witnesses. Into this group fall the insane, imbeciles, idiots, maniacs, the senile, etc. The deaf, dumb and blind, on the other hand, can act as appropriate witnesses provided that they are or have been capable of apprehending through one of the five senses the facts to which they testify in court.[61]

The judge should likewise hear the testimonies of suspected witnesses unsworn. They are: the excommunicated, perjurers and those convicted of infamy, after a declaratory or condemnatory sentence has been inflicted upon them; those of depraved morals and unworthy of trust; and public and grave enemies of either party.[62]

An excommunicated person remains a suspected witness until the excommunication is removed; a person in infamy will continue as such until the Holy See dispenses from the legal infamy or until the ordinary declares that the factual infamy has subsided.[63] On the other hand, a perjurer after a declaratory or condemnatory sentence never ceases to be a suspected witness.[64] Although the Code makes no mention of it an excommunicate who is *vitandus* (even if

[58] Canon 1757, § 1.

[59] Canon 88, § 2.

[60] Schmalzgrueber, *Jus Ecclesiasticum*, Lib. II, Tit. XX, n. 5; Wernz-Vidal, *De Processibus*, VI, n. 466, pp. 402, 403.

[61] Wernz-Vidal, *De Processibus*, VI, n. 466, p. 403.

[62] Canon 1757, § 2.

[63] Noval, *De Processibus*, n. 466, p. 328.

[64] A Coronata, *De Processibus*, n. 1285, p. 194.

he has not been punished with any sentence) should be considered a suspected witness.[65]

The second group of suspected witnesses includes those of such depraved morals that they are unworthy of trust. Canonists have very wisely judged that such individuals could be easily bribed by the unscrupulous to commit perjury.[66] Apparently for the same reason pre-Code authors excluded the poorer classes from acting as witnesses.[67] The Code has rightly done away with this inequitable slur on the poor and has cast her aspersions on those who are poor in morals, not on those who are poor in this world's goods.

Finally, the canons classify public and violent enemies of the litigating parties as suspect witnesses. An enmity would be public if the general populace knew of the ill-feelings which existed between the witness and the litigant, and the circumstances which gave rise to them. An animosity is violent or grave "when it takes rise from a serious cause or is intended to inflict great injury on another's reputation, life or possessions." [68] Witnesses are not rendered suspect after they have reconciled the enmities which existed between themselves and one of the parties in the past.[69] Nor is a witness considered suspect if he is an enemy to both parties in a cause.[70]

Even when the judge excuses a witness from taking an oath he should warn him of the grave obligation incumbent upon him of telling the truth.[71] The judge will do well to emphasize the fact that the witness—even if he gives testimony unsworn—commits a mortal sin if he tells any deliberate falsehood in court. He should lay stress on the lamentable and sometimes appalling consequences which follow from an erroneous sentence based on false depositions. Furthermore, the judge may warn an unsworn witness that falsehood in court may be punished with the dispossession of the rights vested in

[65] Roberti, *De Processibus*, II, n. 337, p. 46.

[66] Augustine, *A Commentary*, VII, pp. 208, 209.

[67] Schmalzgrueber, *Jus Ecclesiasticum*, Lib. II, Tit. XX, n. 28.

[68] Whelan, *The Value of Testimonial Evidence in Matrimonial Procedure*, p. 124.

[69] Wanenmacher, *Canonical Evidence in Marriage Cases*, p. 125.

[70] Note that Canon 1757, § 2, 3°, uses the singular number—"partis."

[71] Canon 1767, § 4.

legitimate ecclesiastical acts.[72] Since those under the age of puberty could scarcely become subject to this penalty [73] the judge need not mention this specific punishment to them.

B. The Refusal of the Witnesses to Take the Oath

As Canon 1767, referring to Canon 1758 cites only two instances in which the judge may omit demanding the oath of the witnesses, it follows that in all other cases he must command them to take it. He should ask even certain non-Catholic witnesses to swear for heretics, schismatics, Jews and in fact all who believe in the one true God can take the oath.[74]

The question is different in the case of atheists, pantheists, materialists and infidels who either allegedly have no belief in a personal God or adore false gods. For such as these, the taking of an oath, which has for its essence the invocation of the one true God to witness the truth, would degenerate into a mere empty and meaningless formula. Again, it must be remembered that to tender the oath to such persons would be to expose the oath, a holy thing, to mockery or ridicule.[75] When these cases arise it is highly advisable for the judge to obtain from the witnesses a solemn promise upon their honor to tell the truth and to consider this promise an equivalent to an oath.

The same practice may be followed in hearing the testimony of those who, like the Quakers and Mennonites, refuse to take an oath on religious grounds. The judge in such instances is shorn, practically speaking, of any coercive powers against them as the witnesses are outside the pale of the Church, and any attempt on the part of the judge to shake the religious convictions which the witness harbors against the taking of an oath would frequently prove to be a sheer waste of time. Furthermore a non-Catholic witness feels usually under no obligation in his own conscience to appear in a

[72] Canons 1743, § 3; 2256, 2°.

[73] Canon 2230: "Impuberes . . . potius punitionibus educativis quam . . . poenis gravioribus vindicativis corrigantur . . ."

[74] *Cf. S. R. R., Osnabrugen, Nullit. Matrim., 11 Jan., 1912, Coram Francisco Heiner, dec. III, n. 6—Decisiones,* IV (1912), 22.

[75] Wernz-Vidal, *De Processibus,* VI, n. 524, p. 472, footnote 3.

court of the Catholic Church and consequently when the non-Catholic is willing enough to testify in a trial, the common rules of courtesy demand that respect and consideration be shown his own religious beliefs and scruples. Hence the judge should give the witness an opportunity to testify to his allegations on his solemn word of honor.

A more difficult problem arises when a Catholic witness refuses to swear. Should he be forced to do so? Canon 1766, § 2, permits the judge to punish such a recalcitrant witness with proportionate penalties, including monetary fines. As the penalties in this instance are indeterminate the judge who wishes to punish a witness for not taking the oath must determine the quality and the quantity of his sanctions from circumstances. For example, a witness who refuses merely to swear should not be punished as severely as one who outright refused to come to court or one who, after he made his appearance in court, refused to give any testimony sworn or unsworn. Again it would scarcely seem equitable to assume that a witness who refuses to take the oath commits as great an offense as one who perjures himself after taking the oath; hence the prudent judge will not inflict on such an individual penalties as severe as those of personal interdict or suspension.

As in the case of a party who refuses the oath, so in the case of a witness who is unwilling to swear, the judge should never fail to inquire into the reasons alleged by him for non-compliance. The witness may refuse to take an oath from motives of sheer obstinacy or contempt of court; if so his action is totally unjustifiable and punishment can be readily meted out to him. On the other hand, it may happen that a witness who promptly obeys a summons to court, who is prepared to answer all the interrogations of the judge and who manifests every sign of respect and docility in a trial may, nevertheless, be unwilling to take the oath because of some scruple of conscience. Far from showing any disrespect or contumacy, a witness may manifest a great regard for the oath by refusing it on the grounds, for example, that his memory is faulty or that he has an inadequate apprehension of the facts about which he is to be interrogated. In such a case it surely seems inequitable to leave the honesty and sincerity of the witness without all recognition and acknowledgment and, contrariwise, to requite the natural manifestations of his over-sensitive conscience with the infliction of ecclesiastical penalties for the sole reason of his refusal to take the oath. In practice the judge may urge a witness of this character to take the oath but he should be extremely slow in punishing him simply for his unwillingness to conform to the rules of the court. The preferable procedure is to avoid making an issue of the refusal of the oath and to hear the witness unsworn.[76]

C. The Value of Unsworn Testimony

It cannot be doubted that testimonial evidence loses much of its probative value when not given under oath. This is evident from Canon 1791, § 2, which specifies that the testimony of two or three absolutely trustworthy witnesses, who give coherent depositions about some matter or event of their own personal observation, *be sworn* before it begets full proof.

What value, it may then be asked, should be placed upon the testimonies of witnesses who refuse to take the oath? Schmalzgrueber [77] and Reiffenstuel [78] give a partial solution for this problem when they state that unsworn testimonies do not furnish even half proof, but such testimonies beget a presumption. Such a presumption has this practical application that, if the proof furnished by both parties is about equal, the judge should decide in favor of the party who has the greater number of unsworn witnesses.

One must subject this more or less absolute rule of pre-Code canonists to certain qualifications. Not only must the judge take into consideration the number of unsworn witnesses; he must weigh the character of unsworn witnesses as well. The following points might aid the judge in estimating the probative value of unsworn testimony:

[76] Roberti, *De Processibus*, II, n. 342, p. 56; *Instructio servanda a tribunalibus dioecesanis in pertractandis causis de nullitate matrimoniorum*, 15 Aug., 1936—Art. 96, § 1, *AAS*, Vol. XXVIII (1936), 333.

[77] *Jus Ecclesiasticum*, Lib. II, Tit. XX, n. 89.

[78] *Jus Canonicum*, Lib. II, Tit. XX, n. 479, *cf*. Bouix, *De Judiciis Ecclesiasticis*, I, p. 313.

1. The person of the witness. Is he a qualified or unqualified witness? As a general rule the unsworn statements of qualified witnesses have more value than those of unqualified witnesses.

2. The character of the witnesses. Are they trustworthy, truthful in their ordinary conversations and honest in their dealings with other men? These facts can be ascertained by testimonial letters or by character witnesses.

3. The quality of the testimony. Do the witnesses answer the questions promptly, readily, unhesitatingly and with a note of assurance? Or do they falter and hesitate when testifying, thereby giving a general impression of uncertainty about the facts to which they bear witness? Did they themselves see or hear the facts to which they testify? Or can they furnish only hearsay evidence? Can they quote the direct words of the party about whom they testify? Or merely a summary of what the party said?

4. The agreement of their testimony with that of other witnesses especially of those who have taken the oath.

D. Mode of Procedure in Administering the Oath

The mode of procedure in administering the oath to witnesses is about the same as that for administering the oath to the parties. The following points peculiar to the oath of the witnesses should be noted. If the promoter of justice or the defender of the bond take part in the trial, they should be present at the taking of the oath. The witnesses may swear singly or in a group; the separate administration of the oath to each witness is the more impressive and expedient procedure.[79] The judge, however, may give his exhortation to the witness collectively. The experts' oath to tell the truth may be combined with the oaths of office and of secrecy into one formula.[80]

[79] Roberti, *De Processibus*, II, n. 343, p. 56.

[80] *Regulae servandae in processibus super matrimonio rato et non consummato*, Appendix n. XXIX.—*AAS*, XV (1923), 432, 433.

CHAPTER VII

THE OATHS OF HAVING SPOKEN THE TRUTH, OF SECRECY, AND OF OFFICE

Article 1. The Oath of Having Spoken the Truth

The oath of having spoken the truth *(jusjurandum de veritate dictorum)* is administered to the witnesses after they have given their depositions. In matrimonial trials and in processes concerning the nullity of sacred ordination the judge must administer this oath to the parties and the experts as well as to the witnesses after he has interrogated them.[1]

In all other trials the judge may tender the oath or omit it as he sees fit.[2] However, prudence would seem to dictate that the judge impose this oath on witnesses in criminal trials for, not unlike marriage processes, they concern the public good. Furthermore, issues of great and grave concern are often at stake in criminal processes and the judge should make every effort to assure himself that his sentence will be in accord with justice and truth. Undoubtedly, the oath of having spoken the truth, offering as it does a further guarantee that the witness speaks the truth can play an important part in assuring the judge that the evidence upon which he must base his sentence harmonizes with objective fact.

The judge cannot impose this oath on the defendant in a criminal trial; [3] nor should he tender it to a witness who is unsuitable or suspect.[4] From the fact that in a private trial the judge should

[1] *Instructio servanda a tribunalibus dioecesanis in pertractandis causis de nullitate matrimoniorum*—15 Aug., 1936, Art. 104, § 2—*AAS,* XXVIII (1936), 335; *Regulae servandae in processibus super nullitate sacrae ordinationis vel onerum sacris ordinibus inhaerentium* editae die 9 Junii, 1931, n. 37—*AAS,* XXIII (1931), 457.

[2] Canon 1768.

[3] Canon 1744.

[4] Canon 1758.

at the request of the parties omit the oath of the witnesses to tell the truth,[5] it does not necessarily follow that under such circumstances he cannot exact from the witnesses the oath of having told the truth. Canon 1768 empowers the judge to demand the oath of having told the truth whenever he deems it prudent to do so; it says nothing about the judge's taking counsel of the parties as to whether it should be tendered or not. This oath is intended to aid the judge in establishing the truth more securely and expeditiously; and it is the judge who can best determine when it should and should not be employed.

One should note that in matrimonial trials and in processes concerning the nullity of sacred ordination, the oath of having spoken the truth covers the entire content of the testimony given and hence cannot be restricted to a few points of the deposition; in all other trials, this oath may embrace the entire testimony which the witness has given or it may be limited to a certain portion of it. The judge will find it particularly advantageous to impose this oath under the following circumstances: (a) when the witness wavered or was uncertain and hesitant in testifying; (b) when one part of his deposition contradicts another; [6] (c) when the testimony of one witness is at variance with another's.[7]

Mode of Procedure in Administering the Oath

After the party, witness or expert has given his full testimony the judge has the notary read aloud the deposition given. He then asks the person examined whether he wishes to add, withdraw, correct or change anything in the testimony. Perfect freedom must be accorded the witness to make any additions, corrections or modifications in his deposition. If the witness answers that he has nothing else to say or to change he takes the oath. The judge is not obliged to admonish the oath-taker of the sanctity of

[5] Canon 1767, § 3.

[6] In such an event the judge after pointing out the contradictions may select that part of the witness's testimony which appears more probable and ask the witness whether he is willing to swear to it.

[7] Roberti, *De Processibus,* II, n. 342, p. 55; Noval, *De Processibus,* Pars I, n. 486, p. 339.

the oath if he has already given his exhortation to that effect.

After taking the oath the party witness or expert signs his testimony. The judge, notary, defender of the bond or promoter of justice (if the latter two officials take part in the trial) must sign after him.[8]

The oath of having spoken the truth is not required for the validity of the testimony. If the oath to tell the truth has been unintentionally overlooked it may be supplied by this oath.

Article 2. The Oath of Secrecy

Canon 1623 treats of two species of secrets which arise in court procedure. The first two paragraphs of this Canon deal with the official secret which binds the judge and the officials of tribunals. The third paragraph describes the sworn secret.[9] This dissertation will limit its discussion to the second type of judicial secret.

The judge can bind witnesses, experts, litigants and their advocates or procurators to sworn secrecy.[10] He may impose the oath of secrecy whenever the trial or the proofs adduced in the trial are of such a nature that from their divulgation (a) the good name of those having no part in the trial is jeopardized or (b) an occasion of quarrels might arise between various individuals or (c) scandal might be given or (d) any grave embarrassment *(incommodum)* might be caused.[11]

Note should be taken of the fact that the judge can oblige the oath-taker to observe secrecy regarding either the whole trial or regarding the questions proposed and answers given. For the sake of clarity the writer will use the term "absolute secrecy" to designate the secrecy that must be observed regarding the *very fact* of the trial; the term "relative secrecy" to designate the secrecy to be observed concerning the questions proposed and answers given in the course of a trial; the term "perpetual secrecy" to indicate that

[8] Canon 1780; *Instructio servanda a tribunalibus dioecesanis in pertractandis causis de nullitate matrimoniorum,* 15 Aug., 1936, Art. 104—*AAS,* XXVIII (1936), 335.

[9] *Cf.* Wernz-Vidal, *De Processibus,* VI, n. 155, p. 133, for this division.

[10] Canons 1623, § 3; 1769.

[11] Blat, *De Processibus,* n. 92, p. 107.

secrecy which must be observed forever; the term "temporary secrecy" to indicate that secrecy which must be observed for a definite period of time—usually until the publication of the process.[12]

In trials which are by nature public—such as marriage trials—the oath of relative secrecy should be tendered to the witnesses, experts, parties and their procurators or advocates.[13] To tender an oath of absolute secrecy in such trials would be ineffective and useless since the fact of the trial is already divulged.

A different problem presents itself when one turns to a consideration of criminal trials. At times the delict of which the accused is charged in criminal processes may be public; at other times it may be occult. It would appear that no particular damage or harm would fall on the accused if it became known that he had been brought to trial for a crime which was of general knowledge among the inhabitants of the district. If the defendant would be found guilty of the delict, the divulgation of the trial and sentence would produce the great moral effect of manifesting to the faithful at large the fact that the Church will not permit her lawbreakers to go unpunished. Far from causing any scandal the divulgation of the trial and sentence will act as an effective weapon in deterring others from a similar grave infraction of the law. On the other hand if the accused is proven innocent of the charges leveled against him the knowledge of the favorable sentence will help to restore his good name and will afford a powerful antidote to the poisonous venom of evil tongues. Hence in public criminal trials the judge does not seem to be obliged to exact the oath of absolute secrecy; but to prevent collusion among witnesses it will generally be good policy to impose the oath of relative secrecy upon those giving testimony.

Turning to occult criminal causes it would appear that the judge

[12] In processes *super matrimonio rato et non consummato* the secrecy must be observed until the adjudication of the process. *Cf. De Processibus in Causis Dispensationis super Matrimonio Rato et non Consummato*, Appendix, XX; likewise in processes concerning the nullity of sacred ordination. *Regulae servandae in processibus super nullitate sacrae ordinationis vel onerum sacris ordinibus inhaerentium* editae die 9 Junii, 1931, Appendix, n. XIX.—*AAS*, XV (1923), 427; *AAS*, XXIII (1931), 485.

[13] *Instructio servanda a tribunalibus dioecesanis in pertractandis causis de nullitate Matrimoniorum*, Art. 104, § 2.—*AAS*, XXVIII (1936), 335.

can prudently tender the oath of absolute secrecy to those giving testimony in them. It is true that the Code nowhere prescribes this regulation but one may logically deduce this principle from the canons which deal with the inquisitorial criminal processes. An inquisition is instituted if a delict is not notorious.[14] This investigation must be shrouded with secrecy lest the good name of the accused or of anyone else be endangered.[15] To obtain this end one can validly suppose that the witnesses who are called upon to testify in the inquisitorial process should take an oath of absolute secrecy. Now if absolute secrecy is demanded in the inquisitorial process can it not be rightfully assumed that the same secrecy should be no less present in *trials* dealing with occult crimes? As long as he is not proven guilty the accused is entitled, in justice, to his good name which would certainly be endangered were the trial to become publicly known. Even if the charges are true the Church will not profit, to say the least, by permitting the delicts of her members to become the common possession of the tale-bearer and scandal-monger. She cannot easily prevent that eventuality whenever the crime of the wrongdoer is of public knowledge; but she can safeguard against it by the oath of absolute secrecy if the crime is occult.

Closely associated with the discussion of the oath of absolute secrecy is the question of the oath of perpetual secrecy. The Code empowers the judge to place parties, procurators, witnesses and experts under the sworn obligation of keeping either trials or facts in a trial a perpetual secret, should he deem that circumstances demand it.[16]

The oath of perpetual secrecy must be imposed on those who testify in a trial involving solicitation.[17] A need of perpetual secrecy might arise in occult criminal causes for reasons cited above. This would probably be all the more true when the penalty imposed for the crime could be paid in an occult manner. The length of time in which the culprit must remain under penalties must likewise be taken into consideration by the judge in determining whether or not to im-

[14] Canon 1939, § 1.

[15] Canons 1943, 1944, § 1; A Coronata, III, *De Processibus*, n. 1464, p. 392.

[16] Canons 1623, § 3; 1769.

[17] Muniz, *Procedimientos Eclesiasticos*, n. 314, p. 250 (1).

pose the oath of perpetual secrecy. For example, a judge could prudently bind to perpetual secrecy all who had part in a trial wherein the defendant was sentenced to lifelong occult penances.

But the circumstances in which the use of the oath of perpetual secrecy is advisable are by no means limited to criminal trials. It is significant that in its recent rules on the trying of matrimonial causes in diocesan courts the Congregation of the Sacraments permits the judge to tender the oath of perpetual secrecy whenever he deems it advisable to do so.[18] It may happen that the judge in the process of interrogating a party, witness or expert will unearth some very occult fact such as a secret murder, a secret act of adultery, a secret revalidation of a marriage, a secret dispensation from an impediment, etc. If he prudently foresees that the revealing of the facts will entail the quarrels, scandals and grave harm referred to in Canon 1623, § 3, he can place the witness or party under perpetual secrecy. It is well to note that a witness can become bound to perpetual secrecy concerning a part of his deposition while remaining bound merely to temporary secrecy about the rest of his testimony.

The formula of the oath of secrecy may be combined with the oath to speak the truth or the oath of having spoken the truth.[19] If it be administered to experts, the oath of secrecy may be united with the oath of office into a single formula.[20] If the oath is one of perpetual secrecy it may be more advisable to tender it under a separate formula in order to avoid ambiguities and to emphasize upon the mind of the oath-taker his solemn obligation of secrecy.

Penalties for Violation of the Oath of Secrecy

The Code has not enacted any penalties against violators of the oath of secrecy. In causes pertaining to the Holy Office, however, officials, parties and witnesses may be obliged to take the oath

[18] *Instructio servanda a tribunalibus dioecesanis in pertractandis causis de nullitate matrimoniorum*, Art. 104, § 2—*AAS*, XXVIII (1936), 335.

[19] Roberti, *De Processibus*, II, n. 343, p. 56.

[20] *Instructio servanda a tribunalibus dioecesanis in pertractandis causis de nullitate matrimoniorum*, Art. 146—*AAS*, XXVIII (1936), 342; *Regulae servandae in processibus super matrimonio rato et non consummato*, Appendix, nn. XXI, XXIX—*AAS*, XV (1923), 427, 432.

of secrecy of that tribunal. Violation of this oath carries with it an excommunication reserved to the Holy Father. This censure is enacted as a *latae sententiae* penalty.[21] This punishment, it should be noted, is incurred by the parties or the witnesses only when they have been forewarned of the penalty at the time of their examination.[22]

From the fact that the Code has not attached any canonical sanctions to the breaking of the oath of secrecy it does not follow that the judge must permit violators to go unpunished. The principles of Canon 2222, § 1, it would appear, may be invoked in this instance. The canon states that when a law has no sanction attached to it, a legitimate superior may punish its transgression with some just penalty, if the scandal given or the gravity of the violation demand it. Now, one can logically assume that in many cases of the violation of the oath of secrecy at least one of the two conditions named in this canon may be present. In not a few criminal causes scandal is an ever-recurring menace, and the avoidance of scandal is one of the reasons why the oath of secrecy is employed.[23] Again, the breaking of the oath may entail the loss of good name to one or both of the parties or the thwarting of justice through collusion among the witnesses—dangers which would certainly justify the assumption that the transgression of the law is grave. In view of these considerations it appears probable that the violators of the oath of secrecy may be punished by the indeterminate sanctions of Canon 2222, § 1.

The question then arises whether the judge can personally inflict punishment or whether he must turn the matter over to the ordinary. Canon 2220, § 1, states that those having judicial power can inflict only those punishments which are specifically stated in the law. In the light of this principle the judge should in practice inform the ordinary of any violation of sworn secrecy and permit him to determine and inflict the penalty.

[21] A Coronata, *De Processibus*, III, n. 531, p. 59.

[22] Lega, *De Judiciis Criminalibus*, n. 531, p. 540.

[23] Canon 1623, § 3: "Imo quoties causae vel probationum natura talis sit ut ex actorum vel probationum evulgatione . . . scandalum . . . oriatur . . ."

Article 3. The Oath of Office

Before undertaking the work which they are called upon to perform for an ecclesiastical court, experts should take an oath of office. Under the term "experts" (*periti*) are included handwriting specialists, interpreters, midwives, physicians and matrons. Theologians and canonists whom the judge may call upon to settle juridic-theological questions arising in a trial are not experts in the strictest sense of that term since their counsel deals more with questions of law or doctrine than with facts which are proved by juridic evidence. As a consequence, they may be exempted from taking the oath of office.[24]

By taking this oath the expert promises to fulfill his office faithfully. More specifically it obliges the expert to perform his work:

(a) *honestly*, by showing neither bias nor discrimination nor prejudice to either of the parties,

(b) *truthfully*, by neither stating falsehoods nor concealing the truth,

(c) *completely*, *i. e.*, by doing his task thoroughly and conscientiously and by avoiding all superficial, careless and slipshod methods in accomplishing his task.

In *matrimonium ratum et non consummatum* processes an interpreter must further promise to translate with care and exactness word for word the acts and documents of the process. Likewise in the same processes the matron in taking the oath of office must give an explicit promise to guard against fraud and to observe the rules of modesty in the corporal examination of the woman.[25]

The experts take the oath of office in the presence of the judge or his delegate. If the promoter of justice or defender of the bond take part in the trial, the judge should summon them to be present at the administration of the oath. The parties should always be permitted to be present at the taking of the oath, for by it the expert enters into a tacit contract with the parties to perform his task.[26] Hence, they should be advised of the place and the date when the ex-

[24] Wernz-Vidal, *De Processibus*, VI, n. 496, p. 437, footnote 20.

[25] *Regulae servandae in processibus super matrimonio rato et non consummato*, Appendix, nn. XXI, XXIX—*AAS*, XV (1923), 427, 432.

[26] A Coronata, *De Processibus*, III, n. 1328, p. 233.

perts are to be sworn into office. The parties cannot remit the oath to the experts by express pact, but they can do so implicitly if, in the event of its omission, they do not bring exception to the testimony of the experts.

The formula of the oath should be signed by the expert, the judge, the defender of the bond or the promoter of justice (if present) and the notary.

If the expert refuses to take the oath of office the judge may, nevertheless, permit him to undertake his work, but the fact of the refusal and the cause alleged should be inserted in the acts.

Penalties for Violation of the Oath

An expert may violate his oath of office by performing his work negligently or fraudulently; by not completing his task within the allotted time; or by avoiding its performance without just cause. An expert who is guilty of such offenses is obliged to make restitution to either one or both of the parties for the damage inflicted upon them by his evil conduct.[27] It is for the judge to decide whether one or both of the parties suffered harm through the malfeasance of the expert and to determine the amount of the compensation to which they are entitled for damages. An expert who committed fraud or deceit in the performance of his work loses all right to remuneration for his services.[28]

Frequently, an expert may be called upon to take an oath to speak the truth or an oath of having spoken the truth in addition to the oath of office. If he then conceals the truth, or states a falsehood, in answering the interrogations put to him the expert is guilty of perjury and can be punished by a personal interdict if he be a layman, or by suspension if he be a cleric.[29] If neither the oath to speak the truth nor the oath of having spoken the truth has been administered, the penalty against an expert giving false evidence in court is restricted to his debarment from the use of the rights implied in the legitimate ecclesiastical acts.[30]

[27] Canon 1798; Noval, *De Processibus,* Pars I, n. 521, p. 359; n. 217, p. 131.
[28] Roberti, *De Processibus,* II, n. 359, p. 84.
[29] Canons 1794, 1743, § 3.
[30] Canons 1743, § 3; 2256, 2°.

CHAPTER VIII

THE PROBATORY OATH

THE Code treats of the probatory oath in Chapter VII of the fourth book from Canon 1829 to Canon 1836, inclusive. The chapter bears the heading *De iureiurando partium*. This title is somewhat ambiguous for confusion might easily arise between the oaths discussed in this section and the oath of the party to tell the truth, which is mentioned in Canons 1744 and 1746. To avoid all possible ambiguities which might arise from a loose use of terms it has been deemed advisable to designate the oaths of Canons 1829-1836 by the expression "Probatory Oaths."

The probatory oaths can be clearly distinguished from the oaths of parties, witnesses and experts to tell the truth and the oaths of secrecy and of office. The latter two oaths affect the proper arrangement of the processual acts. The oath to tell the truth furnishes merely a subsidiary and corroborative mode of proof.[1] The probatory oaths, on the other hand, of themselves supply complete and independent means of proof. To express it succinctly, the oath to tell the truth and the oaths of secrecy and of office pertain to the acts of the process; the probatory oaths pertain to the acts of the cause.[2]

The probatory oath admits of three classifications: the suppletory, estimatory and decisory oaths.

ARTICLE 1. THE SUPPLETORY OATH

Canon 1829 states that if only half proof has been presented in a trial and if no other means of proof are available, the judge can command or permit an oath to be taken to supply the needed proof. The oath thus tendered is called the suppletory oath.

[1] Wernz-Vidal, *De Processibus*, VI, n. 523, p. 471.

[2] Roberti, *De Processibus*, II, n. 380, p. 109.

A. Conditions Required for the Tendering of the Suppletory Oath

1. The party to whom this oath is tendered must be one who has furnished only half proof in the trial. As a consequence of this principle it follows that the judge cannot proffer the oath to a litigant who has fully proved his case. In this instance the judge must pass sentence in favor of the litigant without exacting a suppletory oath from him. This rule was enunciated in the law of the decretals.[3] Furthermore, one of the three requisites for the taking of any oath—judgment[4]—demands the presence of a sufficiently grave reason before the oath is administered. To express this requisite negatively, no one should swear rashly and without need.[5] This need of the suppletory oath can scarcely be admitted if one of the parties furnishes complete proof in the trial.

The use of the suppletory oath, it is evident, requires the judge to make as clear a line of demarcation as possible between full proof and half proof. Hence, a brief digression from the main topic of the dissertation is necessary at this point in order to determine the factors which constitute half and full proof.

> Theoretically, there are two distinct methods of proof appraisal: the purely legal method (systema legale; probatio per legem), and the method of free appraisal (systema morale, intimae persuasionis liberae aestimationis). In the purely legal system of appraisal the law establishes what efficacy the various arguments shall have, and allows no discretion to the judge. In the system of free appraisal, it is left entirely to the prudence or behest of the judge to make of the proofs what he will, and the law in no way limits the use of his discretion.[6]

That the Code combines both methods of proof appraisal is evident from Canon 1791, § 2. The first clause of this canon permits a judge to obtain full proof from the sworn statements of two or three witnesses who are above all exception and who give consistent testimony about some fact of their own knowledge. The second

[3] C. 2, X, *de probationibus*, II, 19.

[4] Canon 1316, § 1.

[5] Schmalzgrueber, *Jus Ecclesiasticum*, Lib. II, Tit. XXIV, n. 5.

[6] Wanenmacher, *Canonical Evidence in Marriage Cases*, pp. 82, 83.

clause of the canon allows a judge to consider such testimony incomplete under certain circumstances. The first clause gives expression to the legal method; the second, to the method of free appraisal. On the one hand, the legislator wished to establish a few general norms for the proper evaluation of proof, so that the ecclesiastical judge would not enter upon his formidable duty of adjudicating cases *clausis oculis,* as Wernz-Vidal aptly express it.[7] On the other hand, the legislator must have realized that so many varying circumstances and so many subjective influences enter into the proper appraisal of proof that to enact unchangeable, inelastic norms which the judge would have to follow in each and every case would be to undertake a task at once futile and impossible. Consequently the decision whether, in a concrete case, complete proof or half proof has been furnished must in the last analysis be left to the prudence of the judge to determine.

However, it may not be amiss to suggest a few examples of evidence which may beget full proof or half proof.

Full proof may be derived from: (1) The sworn testimony of two or three witnesses above all suspicion who give consistent testimony about some fact or facts of their own knowledge; [8] (2) public documents or other writings equivalent to the same; [9] (3) presumption *juris et de jure*; (This presumption has such great probative force that indirect proof alone is admitted against it. [10] The Code mentions but one presumption *juris et de jure*—the presumption which a *res judicata* enjoys); [11] (4) the decisory oath; [12] (5) the judicial confession of a party; [13] (6) evidence or notoriety of fact.[14]

Examples of evidence which may amount to half proof are: (1) the testimony of one witness; [15] (2) private writings; [16] (3) simple

[7] *De Processibus,* n. 482, p. 422.
[8] Canon 1791, § 2.
[9] Canons 1812, 1813.
[10] Canon 1826.
[11] Canon 1904, § 1; Manning, *Presumptions of Law in Marriage Cases,* p. 24.
[12] Canon 1834, § 1.
[13] Canons 1750, 1751.
[14] Canon 2197, 3°.
[15] Canon 1791, § 1.
[16] Canon 1817.

presumption of law; (4) rumor *(fama)* including witnesses *de fama.*[17]

If the judge by prudent appraisal of such evidence believes that half proof has been presented, he may tender the oath to the party who produced the evidence, provided that the other conditions necessary for the suppletory oath are fulfilled.

2. The suppletory oath cannot be tendered in criminal trials.[18] It can be proffered neither to the accused nor to the promoter of justice.

Some pre-Code authors believed that the judge could make use of the suppletory oath in criminal trials of lesser moment in which the penalty inflicted in the event of condemnation was light, *e. g.*, pecuniary fines.[19] Since the Code makes no distinction between criminal trials of greater or minor importance, this opinion of the older authors can no longer be accepted. The use of the suppletory oath is interdicted in *all* criminal trials.

Before the Code several writers forbade the tendering of the suppletory oath to plaintiffs *in causis famosis, i. e.*, contentious trials in which the defendant suffered infamy of fact in the event of condemnation.[20] The distinction between ordinary contentious trials and *causae famosae* has likewise been suppressed by the Code and, as a consequence the prohibition of the suppletory oath extends only to criminal trials in the strictest sense of the term.

3. The suppletory oath is excluded in trials wherein the disputed right or object is of too great a price or the fact of too great a moment.[21] Within the category of such trials could be classified those processes which concern the rights of an entire hereditament or the greater part of one of the litigant's possessions. Generally speaking, however, the prudence of the judge must determine when on this score the oath may be employed and when it must be excluded.[22] In deciding whether or not the disputed right, object or

[17] Wernz-Vidal, *De Processibus*, n. 433, p. 376 (6).

[18] Canon 1830, § 2.

[19] Reiffenstuel, *Ius Canonicum*, Lib. II, Tit. XXIV, nn. 189, 212-214.

[20] Schmalzgrueber, *Jus Ecclesiasticum*, Lib. II, Tit. XXIV, n. 49; Bouix, *De Judiciis Ecclesiasticis*, I, 337.

[21] Canon 1830, § 2.

[22] Reiffenstuel, *Jus Canonicum*, Lib. II, Tit. XXIV, n. 187; Schmalzgrueber, *Jus Ecclesiasticum*, Lib. II, Tit. XXIV, n. 50.

fact is of a value that warrants the exclusion of the oath, the judge must take individual circumstances into consideration. That which might be for one litigant an object of great price may be for another a thing of little value. As a general rule, the greater the value which a party places on a disputed object, the greater will be his temptation to commit perjury in order to obtain that right. The judge must also take into account the probity, the trustworthiness and the honesty of the parties. He should never tender an oath to a person who has been guilty of perjury or even suspected of the same.[23]

4. The suppletory oath must embrace some right, object or fact proper to the litigant to whom the oath is tendered.[24] Hence the facts sworn to must fall within the scope of the oath-taker's knowledge. A possible exception to this rule appears in Canon 1662 which permits a procurator possessing a special mandate to swear in the name of his client. In such a case the procurator must swear in accordance with the formula drawn up by the litigant. As it cannot always be known in advance what circumstances might arise, which render the suppletory oath expedient, the judge should not permit the procurator to take the suppletory oath unless the formula perfectly fits the case at hand.[25]

5. Canon 1830, § 1, suggests that the suppletory oath be employed when facts which pertain to the civil or religious status of a party cannot otherwise be ascertained. This rule is especially true in those circumstances in which the harm or the advantage that results from the suppletory oath accrues to the oath-taker alone.[26]

It is certain that the suppletory oath can be used to furnish evidence that a person is unmarried, baptized, has received orders, has taken vows or is related to some other party. Likewise, the judge can tender it to ascertain facts pertaining to the incardination and excardination of clerics, the loss or acquisition of domiciles and to a cleric's freedom from irregularity and censure.[27]

[23] A Coronata, *De Processibus,* n. 1361, pp. 266, 267.

[24] Canon 1830, § 2.

[25] Noval, *De Processibus,* Pars I, n. 568, p. 380.

[26] Roberti, *De Processibus,* II, n. 381, pp. 110, 111; Wernz-Vidal, VI, *De Processibus,* n. 529, p. 477.

[27] Noval, *De Processibus,* Pars I, n. 568, p. 379; Muniz, *Procedimientos Eclesiasticos,* III, n. 396, p. 327.

The question of whether the suppletory oath can be used in processes concerning the nullity of marriages is a difficult one to solve. A Coronata and Roberti flatly deny the right of a judge to tender the suppletory oath in such trials.[28] They base their contention on the fact that Canon 1830, § 2, interdicts the oath in trials of great importance. Marriage trials, they contend, fall within that category; hence the suppletory oath cannot be employed in them. Wernz-Vidal and Muniz take a more liberal view. They permit the suppletory oath in matrimonial causes to strengthen proofs of the non-consummation of marriage, of the permanence of defective consent, of the permanence of consent in the revalidation of a marriage.[29]

In an analysis of this disputed problem one must begin by drawing an important distinction between a twofold purpose of the suppletory oath. This oath may be used either to settle the main question at issue in a trial or an incidental question which might arise during the course of the process. In the latter case the scope of the oath is restricted to a certain point or number of points in the process which must be disposed of and adjudicated by the judge before he pronounces sentence on the main issue.

Applying this distinction to marriage cases, one can surely say that the use of a suppletory oath, which would cover the whole question at issue in the trial, must be positively prohibited. It would be absurd that a layman, who frequently has little knowledge of the intricate, involved canonical legislation on matrimony, should be given the opportunity of having his marriage declared null and void by the simple expediency of the suppletory oath—even granting that he has furnished evidence which, in the opinion of the judge, might amount to half proof.

The case is different when the oath is restricted to some fact or point in a matrimonial trial. The occasion may not infrequently arise wherein some important point must be settled mainly by the suppletory oath. One can take in the way of an example a trial in which a party wishes to have his marriage declared null on the

[28] A Coronata, *De Processibus*, n. 1361, p. 266; Roberti, *De Processibus*, II, n. 381, p. 110.

[29] Wernz-Vidal, *De Processibus*, VI, n. 529, p. 477; Muniz, *Procedimientos Eclesiasticos*, III, n. 396, p. 327.

grounds of lack of matrimonial consent. Witness after witness may be called into the trial, all of unimpeachable character. They may testify that, judging from this circumstance and that, matrimonial consent was absent. In final analysis, however, the prudent judge will know that only one person in all the world can inform him whether the required matrimonial consent was really lacking—and that person is the litigant himself. The judge, it is true, will usually elicit this information by questioning the party at the commencement of the trial. At times, however, the judge may want double assurance that the petition for the declaration of nullity is founded on the truth before he proceeds to the sentence. In this instance he may again call in the party, after he has heard all the evidence presented, and administer the suppletory oath to him.

That the suppletory oath may be employed in trials pertaining to the nullity of marriages may be proved by the following argument. Canon 1830, § 3, permits the defender of the bond to suggest the tendering of the suppletory oath to one of the parties. This official takes part in those trials which pertain to the bond arising from sacred ordination or marriage.[30] Now if one excluded the suppletory oath from matrimonial bond processes on the score that they are trials of too great a moment to permit the suppletory oath, the defender of the bond could suggest the tendering of the suppletory oath only in those processes which concern the nullity of sacred ordination. It is difficult to concede that a marriage process is of greater moment than a trial pertaining to the nullity of sacred ordination. Hence it seems to be the better view to hold that the suppletory oath can be employed in marriage processes.

Moreover, it is worthy of note that the Sacred Congregation of the Sacraments, while forbidding, in its recent instruction, recourse to the decisory oath in matrimonial trials [31] placed no such restriction on the use of the suppletory oath.

As noted before, the *fact* that a marriage is invalid can never be directly proved by the use of the suppletory oath. However, the suppletory oath may be invoked to substantiate and complement

[30] Canon 1586.

[31] *Instructio servanda a tribunalibus dioecesanis in pertractandis causis de nullitate matrimoniorum*, Art. 1, § 3—*AAS*, XXVIII (1936), 315.

evidence which points to the invalidity of a marriage. Thus in several cases cited by Pallottini the judge tendered the suppletory oath to the wife when the impotence of the husband was not established with certainty. The suppletory oath was likewise employed to establish the fact of fear when perfect proofs of it were unobtainable or where the fear was inflicted occultly.[32] Especial need for this oath may arise in marriage trials wherein the plea for nullity is based on the absence of some internal act required for the validity of a marriage. For example, it may be tendered to a party to substantiate proofs of lack of matrimonial consent; of error; of lack of the required matrimonial intention.[33]

B. Who Can Tender the Suppletory Oath?

The judge alone can tender the suppletory oath. He can do this on his own initiative, or at the request of one of the parties, or at the request of the promoter of justice or of the defender of the bond.[34] If the judge refuses to proffer the oath when the party, defender of the bond or the promoter of justice request it, they can appeal from his decision, provided that their appeal be joined to one from the final sentence, as well.[35]

Ordinarily the petitioning party will request the judge to tender the suppletory oath to his opponent, but the canons do not forbid him to ask that the oath be tendered to himself. Muniz, however, warns the judge to use great circumspection and caution in permitting a petitioner to take the suppletory oath; for in this circumstance the petitioning party assumes the rôle of a voluntary witness.[36]

The petitioner—whether he be a litigant or the promoter of justice or the defender of the bond—should accurately designate the point or question which is to form the subject matter of the oath. The petition should be sent to the opposing litigant to afford him

[32] Pallottini, *Collectio omnium conclusionum et resolutionum S. C. C. ab anno 1564, ad annum 1860*, t. 11, "Juramentum," nn. 3, 4, 6, pp. 103, 104.

[33] Wanenmacher, *Canonical Evidence in Marriage Cases*, pp. 372-376.

[34] Canon 1830, § 3.

[35] Reiffenstuel, *Jus Canonicum*, Lib. II, Tit. XXIV, n. 207.

[36] *Procedimientos Eclesiasticos*, III, n. 397, p. 329.

an opportunity to attack it, if he desires to do so. If he accepts it or if the judge deems his objection to the oath to be unreasonable, the judge issues a decree permitting the oath and containing the formula which is to be sworn to. If he believes that the formula proposed by the petitioner stands in need of correction or revision, the judge has power to make the needed changes.[37]

C. The Time for Tendering the Suppletory Oath

Recourse to the suppletory oath should be had only when other modes of proof are lacking or are insufficient. Hence the judge should not tender the suppletory oath until both parties have presented their proofs and the evidence is closed.[38] If he has given the parties a period for rebuttal he may make use of the suppletory oath after he has heard the plea of the defendant and the allegations of the plaintiff.

Likewise, a party should not request the suppletory oath until both he and his opponent have completed their presentation of evidence, because by petitioning for the oath the litigant renounces his right to furnish other proofs.[39]

D. To Whom Should the Suppletory Oath Be Tendered?

Canon 1830, § 4, states that the judge should usually *(regulariter)* tender the suppletory oath to the party who has furnished the fuller proofs. The word *regulariter* of this Canon permits exceptions to the general rule stated therein, for it may happen that the party who has furnished the more complete evidence will have a less honorable reputation than his opponent. In this instance the judge may tender the suppletory oath to the more trustworthy litigant, even though he has produced the less convincing evidence.[40]

The Code takes no cognizance of those trials in which the proofs offered by the defendant and the plaintiff are about equal.

[37] Wernz-Vidal, *De Processibus,* VI, n. 532, p. 481.

[38] Canon 1860.

[39] A Coronata, *De Processibus,* n. 1361, p. 267.

[40] Roberti, *De Processibus,* II, n. 382, p. 112; Noval, *De Processibus,* Pars I, n. 568, p. 380.

The rules of the Rota of 1910 suggested that in an event of this kind the judge proffer the oath to the defendant.[41] A Coronata believes that in this instance it will generally be more advisable for the judge to refrain from tendering the suppletory oath to either party and to pass judgment in accordance with the principle, *Actore non probante, reus absolvitur.*[42]

This opinion of A Coronata's stands in need of a certain amount of qualification. The general principle, *Actore non probante, reus absolvitur* certainly holds true in trials wherein the entire burden of proof falls upon the plaintiff. But in other processes the defendant must assume the burden of proving his contentions. This may happen in a trial where the adjudication of a disputed right depends on the proving of two facts, the one alleged by the plaintiff to vindicate his right, the other alleged by the defendant to destroy the right of the plaintiff. For example, a plaintiff claims that he has made a certain loan to the defendant. The defendant, in turn, admits the loan but claims that he has paid off the debt. In this case the decision of the trial depends on the payment or non-payment of the debt. The defendant becomes the "proving party," and if he cannot furnish proofs to substantiate his exception to the claims of the plaintiff, he loses the case.

The following rules of Schmalzgrueber will help the judge to determine when the suppletory oath should be tendered to the defendant and when it should be tendered to the plaintiff. Although they are not obligatory, Wernz-Vidal and Muniz suggest them as practical, working norms for the benefit of the judge.[43]

1. If the plaintiff has completely failed to prove his case, the defendant, even if he has furnished no proof in his own behalf, should be absolved without being obliged to take the suppletory oath.

2. If the plaintiff has only a presumption *of fact* in his favor, the suppletory oath should be tendered to the defendant. A pre-

[41] *Regulae servandae in iudiciis apud S. R. Rotae Tribunal,* 4 Aug., 1910, n. 157—*AAS,* II (1910), 830.

[42] *De Processibus,* n. 1361, p. 267.

[43] Schmalzgrueber, *Jus Ecclesiasticum,* Lib. II, Tit. XXIV, nn. 43-46; Wernz-Vidal, *De Processibus,* n. 531, p. 480; Muniz, *Procedimientos Eclesiasticos,* III, n. 396, p. 328.

sumption of fact does not furnish the half proof necessary for the tendering of the suppletory oath.

3. If the plaintiff has furnished half proof, and if the defendant has merely denied the claims of the plaintiff without alleging any proofs in his own behalf, the judge should tender the oath to the plaintiff.

4. If both plaintiff and defendant produce half proof, the oath should be tendered to the defendant except when the great merits and honesty of the plaintiff warrant the judge to assume that he would be more likely to manifest the truth than his opponent.

5. If the plaintiff fully proves his case while the defendant can produce only half proofs, the sentence should be pronounced in favor of the plaintiff and the oath should not be administered to either party. This rule admits of an exception. If the proofs of both parties are not contrary, but reconcilable, the suppletory oath can be tendered to one of the litigants. For example, if the plaintiff fully proves that he has loaned a sum of money to the defendant and if the defendant furnishes half proof that he has paid back the loan, the judge can proffer the oath to the defendant. The principle behind this exception is that the suppletory oath can be offered to a litigant who has half proved some fact against which his opponent has established no proof.

6. If both plaintiff and defendant have fully proved their allegations, the judge must again decide whether the proofs are contrary or reconcilable. If they are reconcilable, sentence should be passed in favor of the defendant without recourse to the oath. If they are contrary the judge should offer the oath to the more trustworthy of the litigants. If they are equally trustworthy, the oath should be tendered to the defendant.

E. The Tendering Back of the Suppletory Oath

The canons offer three alternatives to the party to whom the suppletory oath is tendered: he may take it, or tender it back to the offerer or refuse it.

Before the Code the party could not tender the oath back to

his adversary.[44] The Code has abrogated this restriction and permits the party to tender back the oath to his adversary—regardless of whether the oath was tendered to the party on the judge's own initiative, or at the request of the other litigant, or of the promoter of justice, or of the defender of the bond—provided that the following conditions are fulfilled:

(a) The oath does not concern the civil or religious status of the first party. It would be unfair to offer a suppletory oath which embraces such facts to the second litigant, for ignorance concerning the acts of another person which are not notorious is presumed until the contrary is proved.[45] A suppletory oath which pertains to the civil or religious status of a person will usually center about non-notorious facts; for there will be scarcely any need for a suppletory oath to establish facts which are already notorious.

(b) The conditions necessary for the taking of the suppletory oath must be verified in the second party.[46] For example, the second litigant could not take the oath if he were unable to furnish half proofs.

(c) The judge must give his consent before the first party can tender the oath back to the second party.[47] The judge must decide whether the second party can fulfill the conditions required for the taking of the suppletory oath.

(d) The second party cannot again tender the oath back to the first litigant, but can refuse to take it [48] if he has a just cause.

F. The Refusal to Take the Suppletory Oath

As a general rule, a litigant cannot refuse to take a suppletory oath which pertains to his religious or civil status, for ignorance or error concerning a fact which touches one's own person is not to be presumed.[49] This rule is not without its exceptions. A judge would

[44] *Regulae servandae in iudiciis apud S. R. Rotae Tribunal,* 4 Aug., 1910, n. 158—*AAS,* II (1910), 830.

[45] Canon 16, § 2.

[46] Roberti, *De Processibus,* II, n. 382, p. 110.

[47] Wernz-Vidal, *De Processibus,* VI, n. 533, p. 481.

[48] Noval, *De Processibus,* Pars I, n. 569, p. 381.

[49] Canons 1831, § 1; 16, § 2.

act unjustly were he to demand a suppletory oath regarding some fact which, although it pertains to the party's religious or civil status, falls completely outside the ambit of the party's knowledge. For example, a foundling could not be expected to know at a later period of life whether or not he was baptized by his parents.

A party cannot refuse to take the oath except for a just cause. The absence of any of the conditions required for the tendering of the oath would constitute reasonable grounds for refusing the oath, *e.g.*, if the litigant to whom the oath is tendered has already fully proved his case; if the oath does not pertain to some fact known to the litigant; if the oath concerns some criminal matter; [50] if the oath pertains to a question of very great moment; if the oath is tendered by or to a procurator who lacks a special mandate which empowers him to proffer or take the suppletory oath.[51]

The judge decides whether the refusal to take the suppletory oath is founded on a just cause or whether the refusal is equivalent to a confession.[52] If the judge gives an unfavorable decision, the party who refused the oath can lodge an appeal; hence the notary should carefully record in the acts the reason for the refusal to take the oath.[53]

G. *Recall of the Suppletory Oath*

The judge or the tendering party may recall the oath until it is taken.[54] This might be advisable, for example, if the judge should be given cause to doubt the honesty of the proposed oath-taker or if proofs, hitherto unknown, were unearthed which would render recourse to the suppletory oath unnecessary.

[50] Canon 1743, § 1.

[51] Noval, *De Processibus*, Pars I, n. 569, p. 381. This author believes that a just cause for refusing the oath is also present when the party who *tenders* the oath has not furnished half proof. It is difficult to accept this opinion since the canons do not require the *tendering* party to produce half proof. The requirement of half proof is restricted to the litigant to whom the oath is proffered.

[52] Canon 1831, § 2.

[53] Wernz-Vidal, *De Processibus*, VI, n. 533, p. 481; Reiffenstuel, *Jus Canonicum*, Lib. II, Tit. XXIV, n. 238.

[54] Roberti, *De Processibus*, II, n. 383, p. 112.

H. The Effects of the Suppletory Oath

Since the suppletory oath is intended to complement insufficient proofs, the trial ordinarily comes to a conclusion after it is taken and the sentence is usually passed in favor of the oath-taker. If, however, the judge believes that the suppletory oath has not furnished him with the moral certainty required by Canon 1869, § 1, for passing sentence, he may prorogue the trial and demand other proofs.[55]

I. Attacks on and Appeals from the Suppletory Oath

Canon 1831, § 3, permits a party to attack a suppletory oath taken by his opponent. This attack can be made either in the court of first instance or in a trial of second instance by way of an appeal.[56] The litigant may in order to attack the suppletory oath, employ the same means that are employed to impugn other modes of proof.[57] For example, he could assail the suppletory oath of his adversary by furnishing proofs which would bring to naught the fact or facts supposedly established by the suppletory oath; or by raising a claim that the conditions necessary for the tendering of the suppletory oath were not verified in the case at hand; or by instituting a charge of perjury against the oath-taker.

It is certain that by virtue of Canon 1831, § 3, a party can attack a suppletory oath which the judge on his own initiative has tendered to his opponent; but can a litigant who suggested the tendering of the suppletory oath to his opponent later attack it, after his opponent has accepted his challenge, and taken the oath? A Coronata states that a party who tenders the oath can neither attack it nor make an appeal from its taking. This opinion he modifies by remarking that: " . . . *certe, si (appellatio) admittatur difficile bonum pro appellanti exitum habebit.*" [58] A Coronata quotes Reiffenstuel to sub-

[55] This principle is implied in Wernz-Vidal, *De Processibus,* VI, n. 534, p. 482.

[56] Roberti, *De Processibus,* II, n. 383, p. 112; A Coronata, *De Processibus,* n. 1363, p. 268.

[57] Wernz-Vidal, *De Processibus,* VI, n. 533, p. 482.

[58] *De Processibus,* n. 1363, p. 269.

stantiate his view that a party who tenders a suppletory oath to his opponent loses all right to attack it or to lodge an appeal. Reiffenstuel, as a matter of fact, does state that a litigant who with the approval of the judge has tendered a *juramentum judiciale* to the opposing party, cannot appeal from a sentence based on this oath.[59] However, when Reiffenstuel speaks of the *juramentum judiciale* he refers to the *decisory* oath of the Code and not to the suppletory oath.[60] Hence, A Coronata's argument would seem to be vitiated by an incorrect interpretation of terms; and following the well-known principle of law, *"Ubi lex non distinguit nec nostrum est distinguere"* one can safely say that an appeal may be made against a sentence based on a suppletory oath regardless of whether the oath was tendered on the judge's own initiative or at the request of the party.

J. Mode of Procedure in Administering the Suppletory Oath

Either at the request of one of the parties, or of the defender of the bond, or of the promoter of justice, or on his own initiative the judge issues a decree and admits the oath. The decree determines the oath-taker and contains the points or facts which are to be the subject matter of the oath. The judge cites both litigants, the one to take the oath, the other to attack it if he so desires. The written report should include (a) the formula of the oath, (b) the statement that it was taken or (c) that it was refused or (d) tendered back. If the party refuses the oath the notary should carefully record the reasons for the party's refusal. The report must be signed by the judge, the party and the notary.[61]

Article 2. The Estimatory Oath

The estimatory oath is one which a judge tenders to a party who suffered loss or injury at the hands of the other litigant in order to determine the amount of compensation to which he is entitled.

[59] *Jus Canonicum,* Lib. II, Tit. XXIV, n. 239.

[60] *Cf.* his definition of the decisory oath, Lib. II, Tit. XXIV, n. 135, and of the suppletory oath, Lib. II, Tit. XXIV, n. 138. In pre-Code legislation, the suppletory oath was known as the necessary oath (*juramentum necessarium*), the decisory oath as the judicial oath (*juramentum decisorium judiciale seu juramentum judiciale specifice sumptum*).

[61] Roberti, *De Processibus,* II, n. 384, p. 113.

A. *Conditions Required for the Tendering of the Estimatory Oath*

Canon 1832 lays down two conditions for the tendering of the estimatory oath to the injured party.

1. The right to restitution must be established with certainty. This means that the estimatory oath will have *valid effect* only when one of the parties has proven his right to reparation. It does not imply that a sentence establishing the fact of injury must necessarily precede the administration of the estimatory oath to the plaintiff. In lieu of this procedure the judge, even at the very beginning of the trial, may tender a *conditional* estimatory oath to the allegedly injured party; in this instance the oath will become effective only when the plaintiff has established his claim to restitution. Furthermore, the opposing party can attack the sworn estimate of damages contained in the conditional estimatory oath without having his attack considered as an implicit admission of guilt.[62]

2. The amount of the damage suffered must admit of determination by no other means. This impossibility of determining the damage need not be absolute.[63] Thus the judge may reasonably employ the estimatory oath if he foresees that the hiring of experts will entail a long delay in the trial or will cause considerable expense.

B. *The Tendering of the Estimatory Oath*

The judge must request the party who suffered injury to name under oath the articles which were taken or maliciously destroyed, and to designate their price and value according to a probable estimate.[64] It is evident that the party to whom the estimatory oath is tendered will ordinarily be the plaintiff of the trial. But this is by no means an invariable rule. It might happen in a trial wherein the plaintiff is suing the defendant for recovery of a loan that the defendant will raise the exception that the plaintiff inflicted damages which far exceeded the sum owed by the defendant. In this instance the principle, *Reus excipiendo fit actor* comes into play and the estimatory oath may be tendered to the defendant to permit him, rather

[62] Muniz, *Procedimientos Eclesiasticos,* III, n. 400, p. 332.

[63] Roberti, *De Processibus,* II, n. 386, p. 114.

[64] Canon 1833, 1°.

than the plaintiff, to determine the amount of compensation due.[65]

The judge may tender the estimatory oath on his own initiative or at the request of one of the parties. A party, however, can never directly proffer the oath to his opponent. The approval of the judge is always required.

In Roman Law, from which source it took its origin, the estimatory oath had a penal character. The fact that the defendant upon condemnation was compelled not only to make restitution but to make reparation in terms dictated by the plaintiff as well, constituted in the Roman view a special penalty for the wrongdoer. The Code has apparently stripped the estimatory oath of this penal characteristic.[66] As a consequence, the estimatory oath may be used against a party who inflicted damage unintentionally or retained property in good faith.[67] For the same reason it can be used against an heir of a wrongdoer. Likewise it can be taken by the heir of an injured party or by a minor.[68]

What, it may be asked, is meant by the term "probable estimate" of goods destroyed or taken which as Canon 1833, 1° states, should be determined by the estimatory oath? Pre-Code writers distinguished between three types of estimate: (a) the objective estimate, (b) the estimate *de interesse,* which included the objective estimate, and the profit lost or damages arising from the unjust act and (c) the subjective or sentimental estimate. Following this distinction they divided the estimatory oath into (a) the oath of true estimate, (b) the oath *de interesse* and (c) the oath of affection. Since the Code, the question has arisen whether the probable value of Canon 1833, 1°, should be based on the objective value alone, or on the *interesse* or subjective value of the articles as well. Or, to express it in another way, has the Code abrogated the oaths *de interesse* and of affection?

Wernz-Vidal and Muniz believe that all three types of the estima-

[65] Wernz-Vidal, *De Processibus,* VI, n. 539, p. 486.

[66] Roberti, *De Processibus,* II, n. 386, p. 114.

[67] A Coronata, *De Processibus,* n. 1364, p. 270, remarks: "Ut judex admittat et deferat hoc iusiurandum, de jure Codicis non requiratur dolus in altera parte."

[68] Wernz-Vidal, *De Processibus,* n. 539, p. 486; Roberti, *De Processibus,* II, n. 387, p. 115.

tory oath may still be employed in canonical courts.[69] Roberti implies the opinion that the oath of affection has been abrogated by the Code.[70] Noval readily approves the oaths of true estimate and *de interesse* but definitely interdicts the oath of subjective estimate.[71] A Coronata accepts the oath of subjective estimate since, he states, neither the Code nor the best known canonists exclude it.[72]

It is certain that none of the writers cited above interdicts the use of the oaths of true estimate or *de interesse*. That the oath of true estimate should be permitted in an ecclesiastical court must be taken for granted because the true or objective estimate constitutes the minimum amount which an injured party can claim in the way of compensation.

But in a trial involving restitution the judge must not only observe the requirements of Canon Law in conducting the process, but he must also see that the restitution is performed in accordance with the principles of moral theology. Now, moral theology teaches that a person who has wilfully injured or taken another person's property must make restitution both for the value of the property taken or destroyed, and for the profit lost and damage arising from his unjust act.[73] Since the precise purpose of the oath *de interesse* is to determine both the value of the property taken or destroyed and the amount of profit lost and damage caused, moral theology would seem to give the fullest sanction to its use—granting, of course, that the litigant against whom it is tendered inflicted the damage maliciously or kept the property in bad faith.

Authors disagree on whether the Code has suppressed the oath of subjective value. Noval, who maintains the affirmative view, would seem to hold the better opinion,[74] for it has already been pointed out that the estimatory oath lost its penal character at the time of the

[69] Wernz-Vidal, *De Processibus,* VI, n. 535, p. 483; Muniz, *Procedimientos Eclesiasticos,* III, n. 399, p. 331.

[70] Roberti, *De Processibus,* II, n. 386, p. 114.

[71] Noval, *De Processibus,* Pars I, n. 570, p. 382.

[72] A Coronata, *De Processibus,* n. 1365, p. 270 (8).

[73] Tanquerey, *Synopsis Theologiae Moralis et Pastoralis,* III, nn. 477, 508, pp. 208, 220; Aertyns-Damen, *Theologia Moralis,* I, nn. 754, 763, pp. 490, 495.

[74] *De Processibus,* n. 570, p. 382.

Code; and in pre-Code times the oath of subjective value had as its purpose the infliction of an additional punishment upon the wrong-doer.[75] Hence, if one admits that the estimatory oath no longer retains its penal character, one must likewise grant that the oath of subjective value is suppressed.

The injured party's sworn estimate of damages must not be considered an absolute norm, which the judge must invariably follow in determining the amount of restitution to be made. If he deems the estimate of the party exorbitant, he may reduce it in accordance with the principles of equity, keeping before his eyes all types of evidence and arguments which canonical usage approves.[76]

For example, the judge could require the party to produce conclusive proof that he paid as much for the article as he now claims of the other party. Experts, likewise, may be called in to act as a check on the injured party in establishing a fair and true value of the objects taken or destroyed. They would be especially necessary, it may be remarked, to determine the value of such things as paintings, pieces of sculpture, tracts of land, etc. The proper evaluation of these and kindred objects falls outside the knowledge of the average layman, and, if the ecclesiastical judge does not have recourse to the opinion of experts in such matters, he will be entirely at the mercy of the plaintiff in adjudicating the amount of restitution to be made. This, to say the least, is risky procedure for the virtue of justice obliges the judge not only to secure for the injured party a reasonable amount of restitution, but to protect the culprit from any exorbitant and unjust claims on the part of the plaintiff as well.

Besides the judge, the party who allegedly inflicted the damage may attack the sworn evaluation of the oath-taker. As the oath is ordinarily taken in the probatory period of the trial, he can impugn it in the court of first instance or he can lodge an appeal.[77]

The injured party has the right to refuse the oath and may permit the judge or experts to estimate the amount of restitution that should

[75] Schmalzgrueber, *Jus Ecclesiasticum*, Lib. II, Tit. XXIV, n. 70: "Juramenti affectionis finis est, ut puniatur dolus et contumacia rei rem non restituentis vel non exhibentis."

[76] Canon 1833, 2°.

[77] Wernz-Vidal, *De Processibus*, VI, n. 539, p. 486.

be made.[78] But he never enjoys the personal right of tendering the oath to his opponent.[79]

C. *Mode of Procedure in Administering the Estimatory Oath*

The judge at the request of one of the parties or on his own volition decrees the taking of the oath. His decree should determine the name of the person who will take the oath,[80] the articles whose value is being estimated, and the time and place where the oath is to be taken. The party or his procurator [81] appears before the judge, describes the goods lost or destroyed and determines their probable value by oath. The other party should be cited in order to give him an opportunity to be present. A written record of the oath should always be made and signed by the party, judge and notary.[82]

Article 3. The Decisory Oath

A decisory oath is one which a litigant offers his adversary with the understanding that the question in controversy, whether it be a principal or incidental one, shall be definitely settled by the taking of the oath.[83] Decisory oaths may be divided into judicial and extra-judicial oaths, depending on their administration in or outside of an ecclesiastical trial. This dissertation will limit its discussion to the judicial decisory oath.

Roberti would further divide decisory oaths into necessary and voluntary oaths.[84] A necessary decisory oath, this author says, is one which is prescribed by law; a voluntary decisory oath is one which is suggested by one of the parties. This division of Roberti's seems

[78] A Coronata, *De Processibus*, III, n. 1365, p. 270; Wernz, *Jus Decretalium*, V, n. 648, p. 490.

[79] Roberti, *De Processibus*, II, n. 387, p. 115.

[80] Of course, the oath-taker will always be the party who claims or proves that he has suffered injury. As observed before, this party may be either the plaintiff or defendant in the trial. The decree of the judge should indicate whether the oath-taker is the plaintiff or the defendant.

[81] Canon 1662.

[82] Roberti, *De Processibus*, II, n. 388, p. 115.

[83] Canon 1834, § 1.

[84] Roberti, *De Processibus*, II, n. 389, p. 116.

to lack all foundation in objective fact. In the first place Roberti's division is at variance with the very definition of a decisory oath which clearly demands that *one of the parties* tender this oath. Secondly, in Canons 1628, § 1, and 1764, § 4, which Roberti cites as instances of his necessary decisory oath the judge and not one of the parties tenders the oath to the oath-taker. In neither of these two canons is there any reference made to the decisory oath. Rather, they seem to represent specific applications of the oath of the parties to tell the truth.[85]

Before the Code authors disputed whether the decisory oath was equivalent to a transaction.[86] The Code has vindicated the affirmative opinion.[87]

A. Conditions Necessary for the Tendering of the Decisory Oath

(a) The judge must give his approval.[88] It is he, and not the parties, who is empowered to determine when the conditions required by Canon Law for the tendering of the oath are fulfilled. The judge must not only decree whether or not the oath may be proffered; if he decides in the affirmative he must, as well, accurately determine in his formula the facts which form the subject matter of the oath. He can never command recourse to the decisory oath in a trial; but he is not forbidden to suggest its use if he finds that the necessary conditions are verified. If the judge refuses to permit the administration of the oath, then the party suggesting it has the right of appeal.[89]

(b) The decisory oath must pertain to matters which permit cession and transaction. Without doubt this is the most restrictive of the conditions required for the use of the decisory oath.

The Code does not specify those objects which permit or preclude cession. However, if one follows the opinion of Noval, who practically identifies cession with donation,[90] the restrictions placed by

[85] Canon 1744.

[86] Lega, *De Judiciis Ecclesiasticis*, I, n. 464, p. 410 nota (1).

[87] Canons 1835, 1°, 2°, 3°; 1836, § 2.

[88] Canon 1834, § 1.

[89] A Coronata, *De Processibus*, III, n. 1367, p. 273.

[90] *De Processibus*, Pars I, n. 573, p. 383.

Canon Law on donations can be applied to cessions, as well. Hence, prelates and rectors would be permitted to make only small and moderate cessions from the movable property of their churches in accordance with local customs; cessions involving larger amounts can be made only for a just cause as reward, piety, or Christian charity.[91] Similarly, religious would be forbidden to make cessions from the goods of the house, province, or order save for charitable purposes or for any just cause approved by the superior and in harmony with the norms of the constitutions.[92]

Applying these principles to the use of the decisory oath, it follows that, in trials involving the movable property of their churches, prelates and rectors can ordinarily take or tender the decisory oath only when the sum in dispute is small. However, a trial which centers around the payment of a salary and which involves a large sum can be settled by the decisory oath, because Canon 1535 permits more important donations to be made for purposes of remuneration. In trials which concern the goods of their institute, religious may tender or take the decisory oath with the permission of their superiors, and provided the amount in dispute does not exceed the sum fixed by the constitutions for donations.

A transaction may be defined as an onerous contract about a doubtful matter by which the parties, through mutually giving, retaining or promising something, put an end to a dispute which has arisen and which as yet has not been settled, or prevent a dispute which may or might arise.[93]

A decisory oath fulfills the requirements of a valid transaction. On the one hand, the party tendering the oath renounces his right of action, if his opponent accepts the oath. On the other hand, the party accepting the oath makes a concession by assuming the burden and responsibility involved in the act of swearing. The mutual concession contained in the decisory oath has for its direct object not the

[91] Canon 1535.

[92] Canon 537.

[93] Lega, *De Judiciis Ecclesiasticis*, I, n. 6, p. 28; Noval, *De Processibus*, n. 719, p. 468.

thing controverted, but the determination of the *manner* in which the dispute will be settled.[94]

Transaction (and, as a consequence, the decisory oath) is forbidden:

1. In criminal trials.[95] This prohibition does not extend to contentious cases for damages resulting from a crime.[96] Such cases permit of settlement by transaction, provided that it is strictly limited to the parties themselves. It can never be employed by the promoter of justice.[97]

2. In trials involving the dissolution of the matrimonial bond. This prohibition has been reiterated in recent norms of the Congregation of the Sacraments which state that cases concerning the matrimonial bond cannot be settled by transaction, arbitration or the decisory oath.[98] However, transaction is permitted in separation causes provided that the parties abide by the other canonical requirements.[99] Those who have reached the age of puberty may use the process of transaction to sever espousals of doubtful validity; and nothing prevents them from settling damages resulting from broken engagements by the same means.[100]

3. In trials concerning the title to a benefice. Thus two priests who both lay claim to the pastorate of a parish cannot settle their dispute by transaction or a decisory oath. Nevertheless, Canon 1927, § 1, allows transaction in this case if the lawful authority gives its consent to the settlement by transaction. The canon does not specify the persons embraced by the term *legitima auctoritas*, but it appears

[94] Lega, *De Judiciis Ecclesiasticis*, I, n. 464, p. 410, nota 1. His opinion is accepted by Roberti, *De Processibus*, II, n. 389, p. 116; Wernz-Vidal, *De Processibus*, n. 543, p. 492 nota (56); and A Coronata, *De Processibus*, n. 1366, p. 271, nota 4.

[95] Canon 1927, § 1.

[96] A Coronata, *De Processibus*, III, n. 1445, p. 369.

[97] Wernz-Vidal, *De Processibus*, VI, n. 669, p. 617.

[98] *S. C. de Sacr., instr. servanda a tribunalibus dioecesanis in pertractandis causis de nullitate matrimoniorum*, 15 Augusti, 1936, Art. 1, § 3—*AAS*, XXVIII (1936), 315.

[99] Canons 1128-1132; Noval, Pars I, *De Processibus*, n. 725, p. 474.

[100] Wernz-Vidal, *De Processibus*, VI, n. 668, p. 615.

logical to assume that the phrase refers to the person, physical or moral, who has the right to confer the benefice.[101]

4. In spiritual matters whenever the payment of a temporal thing is involved. This restriction seems to be a particular application of the canons which forbid simony; for transactions in spiritual matters involving the payment of a temporal thing certainly must be considered in the light of Canon 727, § 1, simony which is contrary to the prescriptions of divine law.

Hence transactions are forbidden in disputes involving the administration of the sacraments and sacramentals, the exercise of ecclesiastical jurisdiction, the granting of indulgences, the bestowal of consecrations and blessings, the right to receive tithes, and the rights of presentation, patronage and of canonical provision.[102]

Not all material ecclesiastical goods even though they be united to spiritual things, preclude the use of transaction. Canon 1927, § 2, permits transaction in the case of temporal ecclesiastical goods and objects which, although connected to spiritual entities, are separable from them. If one compares Canon 1927, § 2, with Canon 730, a definite parallel can be established between the two laws. Canon 730 declares that no simony exists in the exchange of a temporal object for another temporal object which, although united to something spiritual, can be considered apart from it. Since simony is not present in such instances, transaction can be invoked to compromise disputes which may center about such temporal objects. For example, two clerics may by transaction determine the ownership of a consecrated chalice provided that they prescind from the fact of its consecration. Likewise, disputes about the fruits of a benefice may be decided by transaction.[103]

[101] *Cf.* Canons 1431-1435.

[102] Noval, *De Processibus,* Pars I, n. 725, p. 474; Wernz-Vidal, *De Processibus,* VI, 668, p. 615.

[103] Wernz-Vidal, *De Processibus,* VI, n. 668, p. 615; Lega, *De Judiciis Ecclesiasticis,* I, n. 10, p. 34. Noval (*De Processibus,* n. 726, p. 475) would exclude the *bona sacra* of Canon 1497, § 2, from the possibility of transaction. This exclusion seems to be too wide, for under the *bona sacra* of Canon 1497, § 2, are included not only temporal objects which are inseparably united to spiritual things, but those which are *separably* united as well. In the following sentence Noval admits that temporal objects which are *separably* associated with spiritual things allow of transaction.

A settlement of a dispute by transaction must not do violence to the principles of alienation of Church goods.[104] Hence, if the value of the objects to be transacted is of an amount which demands the consent of higher ecclesiastical authority for its alienation, this consent must be obtained before the transaction is entered upon.[105]

Ecclesiastical law has canonized the civil law of transactions for Canon 1926 prescribes that in an ecclesiastical transaction the civil laws of the state in which the process takes place must be observed, provided they are not opposed to divine ecclesiastical law. Canon 1926 seems to be an extension of Canon 1529, which states that whatever the civil law of a country determines with regard to contracts, general and specific, nominate and innominate, and to payments shall be observed also in ecclesiastical law and with the same legal effects, unless the civil law runs counter to divine law and unless the canons provide otherwise.

(c) The object of the decisory oath must not be of too great importance or value to the litigants.[106] Probably, the cause underlying this restriction is the presumption that the greater the value or importance of the object at stake, the greater will be the temptation of the parties to commit perjury to obtain the object. No iron-clad norms can be laid down to determine when the thing in dispute is of too great a value or importance to permit the decisory oath. The decision as to when the oath may be admitted and when it must be rejected on this score must be left to the prudence of the judge. It may not, however, be amiss to note that the character and status of *both* parties must be taken into consideration by the judge in arriving at his decision.[107] This follows from the fact that the party to whom the decisory oath is proffered may tender it back to the offerer; and consequently the judge cannot tell in advance which of the litigants will take the oath.

The judge must weigh the character of the parties as well as

[104] Canon 1927, § 2.

[105] For a complete and scholarly treatment of alienation, see Cleary, *Canonical Limitations on the Alienation of Church Property*, Washington, D. C., 1936, pp. 58 ff.

[106] Canon 1835, 1°.

[107] Wernz-Vidal, *De Processibus*, VI, n. 542, p. 489.

their financial status in deciding upon the admission or rejection of the oath. If both are of excellent, unimpeachable character a more important issue can be decided by the decisory oath than if one or both parties have a shadowy or suspicious reputation. The oath should not be permitted when one of the parties committed perjury in the past. Nor should the judge permit the parties to settle their dispute by decisory oath when the value of the object exceeds the limit set by civil law for transactions.[108]

(d) The party who tenders or accepts the decisory oath must have the power to cede or transact.[109]

To have the power to cede, the party must have full capacity of disposing of his rights.

Excluded from transacting and hence from taking or tendering the decisory oath are the following:

1. Those who are habitually destitute of the use of reason, such as infants, the insane and the feeble-minded.[110] Those under fourteen cannot enter into a judicial transaction since they are not permitted to take part in a trial.[111] Minors between the ages of fourteen and twenty-one may tender or take the decisory oath in court, but prudence demands that the judge forbid this if the minors have not received the necessary consent of their guardians. Procurators who represent the insane, the feeble-minded, infants and minors in court may tender or take the decisory oath if they have a special mandate that empowers them to transact in the name of their clients.

2. Local ordinaries, religious superiors and rectors of churches whenever the dispute pertains to the goods of the Church. These officials can enter into a transaction only when a just cause is present and the solemnities required for alienation are observed.[112]

3. Religious without the consent of their superiors.

4. Procurators who lack a special mandate permitting them to transact.

(e) The decisory oath cannot be tendered to a litigant who has

[108] Noval, *De Processibus*, Pars I, n. 573, p. 383.

[109] Canon 1835, 2° and 3°.

[110] Lega, *De Judiciis Ecclesiasticis*, I, n. 9, p. 31.

[111] Canon 1648, § 1.

[112] Wernz-Vidal, *De Processibus*, VI, n. 666, pp. 612, 613.

furnished full proof.[113] Judgment, one of the three conditions for the licit tendering of an oath, requires that the oath should be administered only when a real need of it exists. A need for an oath cannot be admitted when one of the parties has fully proved his case; its use under such circumstances is unnecessary and to no purpose.

One should take note of the fact that the decisory oath, unlike the suppletory oath, can be employed when less than half proof or even when no proof its furnished by the parties. Before the Code the question was mooted whether a plaintiff who furnished no proof, could tender the decisory oath to the defendant.[114] The Rules of the Rota required that both parties furnish some proof at least before the decisory oath was invoked.[115] The Code has not retained these restrictions on the decisory oath, and for this reason it can receive far wider use than hitherto.

The principles of the decisory oath in its relation to the presentation of proof may be summarized as follows:

1. The decisory oath cannot be tendered to a party who has fully proved his case.

2. The decisory oath can be employed when both parties furnish equal proof.[116]

3. The decisory oath can be tendered to a party who has furnished no proof or less than full proof.[117]

4. The decisory oath can be tendered by a party who has furnished no proof or less than full proof.[118]

(f) The oath must concern either the mere knowledge of a fact, or a fact which is proper to him to whom the oath is tendered.[119] Here again one sees a difference between the conditions for a suppletory oath and those for a decisory oath. A suppletory oath must always concern a fact proper to the oath-taker. The corresponding

[113] Canon 1835, 3°.

[114] Schmalzgrueber, *Jus Ecclesiasticum*, Lib. II, Tit. XXIV, nn. 25-30.

[115] *Regulae servandae in iudiciis apud S. R. Rotae Tribunal*, 4 Aug., 1910, n. 150—*AAS*, II (1910), 829.

[116] A Coronata, *De Processibus*, III, n. 1367, p. 272.

[117] Wernz-Vidal, *De Processibus*, VI, n. 542, p. 489.

[118] Roberti, *De Processibus*, II, n. 390, p. 117.

[119] Canon 1835, 4°.

condition for a decisory oath is wider in comprehension. A decisory oath may concern a fact proper to the oath-taker or it may embrace a knowledge of some fact regardless of whether that fact is proper to the oath-taker or not.[120] The Rules of the Rota of 1910 observe that there is especial need for a decisory oath concerning a knowledge of some fact when the oath-taker (as for example the moderator or administrator of a college or pious foundation) alone has knowledge of the fact in dispute.[121]

The swearer may have obtained his knowledge either directly or indirectly.[122] In the first case the oath would be one *de scientia;* in the second case, an oath of belief.

This condition does not exclude a procurator from taking or tendering a decisory oath provided that he has a special mandate.[123] Representatives of moral persons, on the other hand do not need a special mandate to swear or to offer the oath.[124]

B. Revocation of the Decisory Oath

Canon 1836, § 1, permits the party offering the oath to recall it as long as the other party has not taken it or tendered it back. The party can recall the oath even after the decree of the judge permitting the oath has been issued.[125] The Code does not prohibit the party who recalled it from again requesting the oath in the course of the trial. The formula of the oath when suggested the second time may be altered or it may remain unchanged.

C. The Tendering and the Taking of the Decisory Oath

The tendering of the decisory oath consists in an agreement, suggested by one litigant to the other, that with the approval of the judge the question in the trial (either principal or incidental) shall

[120] The adjective *proprium* of Canon 1835, 4°, modifies the word *facto* and not *notitia facti.*

[121] *Regulae servandae in judiciis apud S. R. Rotae Tribunal,* 4 Aug., 1910, n. 150—*AAS,* II (1910), 829.

[122] Roberti, *De Processibus,* II, n. 390, p. 118.

[123] Noval, *De Processibus,* Pars I, n. 573, p. 384.

[124] A Coronata, *De Processibus,* III, n. 1367, p. 272.

[125] A Coronata, *De Processibus,* III, n. 1367, p. 273.

be definitely settled by oath. The party proposing the oath should write out his petition which is to contain (a) the request for the oath, (b) the formula of the oath, and (c) the reasons why his petition is in accordance with the law. The judge examines the petition. If he is satisfied that the necessary conditions are verified and that the party to whom the oath is tendered is an honest individual, he should accept the petition, notify the other party of his acceptance and determine a period of time within which the second party must decide whether to take the oath, or tender it back, or furnish just cause for refusing it. The second party has the right to suggest changes in the formula. If the two parties do not agree on the formula, or if the judge deems it vague, ambiguous or deceitful, he may modify it. The parties should accept the formula thus suggested by the judge.[126]

The oath is considered accepted when the second party declares that he is prepared to swear to the formula proposed by his adversary and admitted by the judge. Once the party accepts the oath he is bound to take it and cannot tender it back to his adversary.[127] He should take the oath in the presence of his opponent.

When the oath is taken the question is decided in accordance with the sworn formula as if judicial cession or transaction had taken place.[128] The judge is obliged merely to confirm by his sentence or decree the fact which has been decided by the oath. He is under no obligation to investigate whether the oath is false or true. No appeal is granted from a sentence based on the oath.[129] It becomes a *res judicata* [130] and enjoys the favor of a presumption *juris et de jure*.[131]

D. *The Refusal to Take the Decisory Oath*

The party to whom the decisory oath is tendered faces three possible alternatives: he may take the oath and thus win the case or the point around which the oath centers; he may tender it back

[126] Wernz-Vidal, *De Processibus*, VI, n. 543, p. 490.
[127] Roberti, *De Processibus*, II, n. 391, p. 118.
[128] Canon 1836, § 2.
[129] Canon 1880, 5°.
[130] Canon 1902, 3°.
[131] Canon 1904.

to the proposer; or he may refuse it. Canon 1836, § 3, considers the last of these three alternatives. The judge, it says, must evaluate the fact of the refusal to swear. He must decide whether the party has just cause for refusal; if not the refusal must be considered as equivalent to a confession; the refusing party then loses the case or that particular point which is the subject matter of the oath.[132]

To furnish an adequate cause for refusing the oath, then, is of supreme importance to the party who refuses the oath. A sufficient reason would be present if the party could show that one of the conditions necessary for the decisory oath is lacking, *v. g.*, if the question in dispute is of too great importance to permit the decisory oath, if the party had no power to transact, etc. The decision as to whether the cause alleged was actually present or whether it was founded on truth must be left to the judge.

E. The Tendering Back of the Oath

The litigant to whom the oath is offered has the option of tendering it back to the offerer. He cannot do this directly; he must first petition the judge and gain his approval to the referring (relation) of the oath. The judge should carefully examine the merits of the case to ascertain whether the necessary conditions of a decisory oath are verified in the person of the offering party.[133] He must exercise especial care that the offerer of the oath verifies the fourth requirement of Canon 1835, for it not infrequently happens that both parties do not have common knowledge about the same fact. If the judge is satisfied that the offerer is fully qualified to swear, he must permit the second party to tender the oath back to him. If the offerer refuses to take the oath when tendered back to him he loses the case or the point which forms the object of the oath.[134] This canonical principle would seem to follow from the dictates of equity, for it is unjust for one litigant to impose upon the other party a burden which he himself is loath to accept.[135]

[132] Noval, *De Processibus*, Pars I, n. 574, p. 384.

[133] Canon 1836, § 5.

[134] Canon 1836, § 4.

[135] As expressed in the Digest: "Non deberet displicere condicio iurisiurandi ei qui detulit."—D. (12.2) 34.

What is the consequence if the judge decides that good reasons exist for not permitting the oath to be tendered back? The authors do not discuss this possibility. It would seem logical to assume that the trial would continue and other modes of proof, such as witnesses, documents, etc., must be resorted to in lieu of the decisory oath. The judge cannot forthwith condemn the litigant to whom the oath was tendered; for, instead of refusing the oath he has availed himself of one of the two alternatives permitted to him by the law—that of tendering it back. Neither can the offerer be condemned for in the case in question he has no opportunity of taking it or refusing it.

F. *Appeals From the Decisory Oath*

To understand the proper relationship of the decisory oath to the question of appeal one should note carefully the wording of Canon 1880, 5°: "Non est locus appellationi. . . . A definitiva [sententia] quae iureiurando litis decisorio innixa est." A sentence, then, which is based on a decisory oath must be a definitive (or in other words the principal) sentence before it becomes a *res judicata,* which precludes appeal. Does it follow that an interlocutory sentence based on the decisory oath can be appealed? In answering this question n. 6 of Canon 1880 must be taken into consideration. An interlocutory sentence can be appealed provided the appeal is joined to an appeal from the definitive sentence. For example, an incidental question is decided by a decisory oath while the definitive sentence is given by the judge without any recourse to the decisory oath. In this instance both the definitive sentence as well as the incidental question settled by oath can be appealed.

Furthermore, the definitive sentence which Canon 1880, n. 5 excludes from the possibility of appeal must be based on the *taking* of the decisory oath. Hence it follows that if the final sentence is appealed, an appeal can likewise be lodged against the following interlocutory sentences of the judge:

(a) The ruling of the judge prohibiting the use of the decisory oath.

(b) The ruling of the judge who denies that just reasons are present for refusing the oath.[136]

[136] Canon 1836, § 3.

(c) The ruling of the judge who forbids the tendering back of the decisory oath.[137]

If the judge of the appellate court confirms the sentence of the judge of first instance the question becomes a *res judicata* [138] and no further appeal can be granted.[139]

Since a definitive sentence based on the taking of a decisory oath enjoys the status of a presumption *iuris et de iure* [140] no direct proofs can be alleged against it. Indirect proofs, on the contrary—proofs which attack the fact which forms the basis for the presumption—may be admitted.[141] Thus if the party who loses a case settled by the decisory oath finds evidence to show that the oath-taker committed perjury he could institute a criminal charge against him. If the suspected party is proved guilty of perjury either by judicial sentence or by a confession [142] the injured litigant has a right to seek a *restitutio in integrum* against the sentence based on the perjured decisory oath.[143] The *restitutio in integrum* revokes the sentence which has been proven unjust [144] by the perjury of the oath-taker.

G. Mode of Procedure in Administering the Decisory Oath

The decisory oath is permitted at any stage of the trial even in the appeal.

The party who takes the oath appears before the judge on the appointed day and hour and pronounces the oath according to the stated formula. The judge should notify the other party or his procurator of the taking of the oath to afford him the opportunity to be present if he so desires. A written report of the tendering or the tendering back, or the taking or refusal (with causes alleged) of the

[137] Canon 1836, § 5.

[138] Canon 1902, 1°.

[139] Canon 1880, 4°.

[140] Canons 1880, 5°; 1902, 1904, § 1.

[141] Canon 1826.

[142] Reiffenstuel, *Jus Canonicum*, Lib. II, Tit. XXIV, n. 156.

[143] Canon 1905, § 2, n. 3; A Coronata, *De Processibus*, III, n. 1368, p. 274 (7); Lega, *De Judiciis Ecclesiasticis*, I, n. 465, p. 412.

[144] Canon 1689.

oath should always be drawn up by the notary. This report should indicate the names of the parties who tendered or tendered back or took or refused the oath; the formula of the oath; the judge who received it; the persons present; the time and place where the proceedings took place. It should be signed by the oath-taker, the judge and the notary.[145]

[145] Canon 1642, § 1; Roberti, *De Processibus*, II, n. 393, p. 120.

THE EXHORTATION OF THE JUDGE TO THE OATH-TAKER

Before I administer the oath to you, I wish to call your attention to the grave and serious responsibility which its taking entails.

The oath is a most sacred act of religion by which you call upon the all-holy and all-truthful God to witness the truth of what you say. By taking it, you transport yourself in spirit out of the presence of an earthly judge, subject to error, and into the presence of Him Who will one day judge your innermost thoughts, words and deeds. It is He and not a mere human creature like myself to whom you make your solemn promise to speak the truth.

Consider for a moment the import of that promise you make to your God. In taking the oath, you promise that you will speak the whole and entire truth in answer to the interrogations put to you; that you will give your testimony, uninfluenced by any motives of love, hate, favor, or financial gain; that you will not knowingly permit the slightest shred of falsehood to enter into your deposition.

Consider, furthermore, the many sad and lamentable consequences which follow from the sin of perjury. Even if no human eye shall discern his sin, the perjurer knows that he has committed a most grievous offense against his God. By his sinful act the perjurer makes a hideous mockery out of God's holy Name in calling upon the all-truthful One to bear witness to a falsehood. He merits the severest condemnations of an outraged Godhead. But the perjurer sins grievously not only against the law of God; he breaks an important commandment of God's holy Church as well.

To Laymen:

If his crime be discovered, a perjurer must suffer the penalty of a personal interdict. This punishment deprives him of one of the highest privileges that a Christian in this life may enjoy—the privilege of attendance at divine services in a Church. If he departs from this life with the interdict upon his soul, he is deprived of the right of Christian burial.

To Clerics:

If his crime be discovered, a perjured cleric must suffer the penalty of suspension. This punishment deprives him of the exercise of the highest prerogatives which adorn the clerical state—namely the celebration of or ministration at Holy Mass, and the administration of the Sacraments.

In Marriage Trials:

Consider the especial gravity of the sin of perjury in a matrimonial trial. If, relying on the depositions of a perjured witness, the judge should pronounce a marriage invalid which is really valid that witness is guilty of the awful sin of sacrilege. If the parties, believing themselves free from the matrimonial bond, should enter into another marriage before the Church, this new marriage is actually invalid and thus the putative husband and wife, and any children they may have, will be involved in an almost inextricable tangle of grievous consequences.

Such, then, are the dire effects which may flow from perjured depositions.

BIBLIOGRAPHY

Sources

Acta Apostolicae Sedis (AAS), Romae: Typis Polyglottis Vaticanis, 1909-

Codex Iuris Canonici Pii X Pontificis Maximi iussu digestus Benedicti Papae XV auctoritate promulgatus, Romae: Typis Polyglottis Vaticanis, 1918.

Codicis Iuris Canonici Fontes, cura Emi. Petri Card. Gasparri editi, 7 vols. Romae: Typis Polyglottis Vaticanis, 1923-1933.

Collectanea S. Congregationis de Propaganda Fide, 2 vols. Romae, 1907.

Concilii Plenarii Baltimorenses III (1884), *Acta et Decreta*, Baltimorae: Typis Joannis Murphy et Sociorum, 1886.

Corpus Iuris Canonici, Editio Lipsiensis II, Richter-Friedburg, 2 vols., Lipsiae, 1922.

Corpus Iuris Civilis, 3 vols., Berlin, 1928-1929.

Institutiones, quas recognovit P. Krueger.

Digesta, quae recognovit T. Mommsen et retractavit P. Krueger.

Codex Iustinianus, quem recognovit et retractavit P. Krueger.

Novellae, quas recognovit R. Schoell et absolvit G. Kroll.

Decretales D. Gregorii IX, una cum Glossis Restitutae, Romae, 1582.

Decretum Gratiani emendatum et notionibus illustratum una cum glossis, Gregorii XIII Pont. Max. iussu editum, 2 vols., Romae, 1582.

Fontes Iuris Romani Antejustiniani in Usum Scholarum, ediderunt S. Riccobono, J. Baviera, C. Ferrini, Iuris Antecessores Leges, Auctores, Leges Saeculares. Florence: S. Barbera, 1908. Gaii Institutionum Commentarii Quattuor Iulii Pauli Quinque Sententiarum ad Filium.

Mansi, Joannes, *Sacrorum Conciliorum Nova et Amplissima Collectio*, Joannes Dominicus Mansi et post ipsius mortem Florentius et Venetianus Editores, 53 vols., Paris: Welter, 1901.

Migne, Jacques Paul, *Patrologia Latina*, 221 vols., Paris, 1847-1870.

Monumenta Germaniae Historica, Leges, Georgius Henricus Pertz edidit, 5 vols., Hanover, 1925-1929.

Pallottini, S., *Collectio Omnium Conclusionum et Resolutionum Apud Sacram Congregationem Cardinalium Sacri Concilii Tridentini*, 17 vols., Romae, 1886.

Regulae Servandae in Iudiciis Apud Sanctae Romanae Rotae Tribunal, Romae: Typis Polyglottis Vaticanis, 1910.

Regulae Servandae in Processibus Super Matrimonio Rato et non Consummato, Romae: Typis Polyglottis Vaticanis, 1923.

Regulae Servandae in Processibus Super Nullitate Sacrae Ordinationis vel

Onerum Sacris Ordinibus Inhaerentium, Romae: Typis Polyglottis Vaticanis, 1931.

Sanctae Romanae Rotae Decisiones seu Sententiae, 20 vols., Romae: Typis Polyglottis Vaticanis, 1912-1930.

WORKS OF REFERENCE

A Coronata, P. Matthaeus Conte, *Institutiones Iuris Canonici Ad Usum Utriusque Clerici et Scholarum*, 3 vols., Vol. III, *De Processibus*, Taurini: Marietti, 1933.

Aertyns-Damen, *Theologia Moralis*, 2 ed., 2 vols., Taurinorum Augustae: Marietti, 1928.

[Bachofen], Charles Augustine, O.S.B., *A Commentary on Canon Law*, 4 ed., 8 vols., St. Louis: B. Herder Book Co., 1920.

Berardi, Carolus Sebastinus, *Gratiani Canones Genuini ab Apocryphis Discreti*. 3 vols. in 4, Venetiis: Ex Typ. P. Valnasensis, 1777.

Blat, Albertus, *Commentarium Textus Codicis Iuris Canonici*, 6 vols., Vol. IV, *De Processibus*, Romae: Ex Typographia Pontificia in Instituto Pii X, 1921-1927.

Bouix, Marie Dominique, *Tractatus De Iudiciis Ecclesiasticis*, 3 ed., 2 vols., Paris, 1883.

Buckland, W. W., *A Textbook of Roman Law from Augustus to Justinian*, 2 ed., Cambridge: Cambridge University Press, 1932.

Catholic Encyclopedia, The, 15 vols., New York: Robert Appleton Co., 1917.

Cleary, Joseph F., *Canonical Limitations on the Alienation of Church Property*, The Catholic University of America Canon Law Studies, Number 100, Washington, 1936.

Colinet, Paul, *La Procédure Par Libelle*, Études Historiques Sur Le Droit De Justinien, Tome Quatrème, Paris: Librarie Du Recueil Sirey, 1934.

Conran, Edward James, *The Interdict*, The Catholic University of America Canon Law Studies, Number 56, Washington, 1930.

Continental Legal History Series, The, 10 vols., Boston, 1927. Vol. VII, Engelmann, Arthur, *A History of Continental Civil Procedure*, trans. R. W. Millar.

Demelius, *Schiedseid und Beweiseid im Römischen Civilprozesse*, Berlin, 1887.

Durandus, Gulielmus, *Speculum Iuris*, Venetiis: Apud Iuntas, 1577.

Eichmann, Eduard, *Das Prozessrecht des Codex Iuris Canonici*, Paderborn: Ferdinand Schöningh, 1921.

Haring, Johann, *Der Kirchliche Eheprozess*, Graz: Ulrich Moser, 1929.

Jobbe-Duval, Emile, *Études Sur L'Histoire de La Procedure Civile Chez Les Romains*, Paris: Librairie Nouvelle de Droit et de Jurisprudence, 1896.

Lega, Michael, *Praelectiones In Textum Iuris Canonici De Iudiciis Ecclesiasticis In Scholis Pont. Sem. Rom. Habitae*, 4 vols., Romae: Ex Typographia Polyglotta S. C. de Propaganda Fide, 1905. Vol. I, *De Judiciis Ecclesiasticis Civilibus*, 3 ed., Romae, 1905. Vol. IV, *De Iudiciis Criminalibus In Genere Et In Specie De Delictis Et Poenis Praemisso Tractatu*, Romae, 1901.

Manning, John J., *Presumption of Law in Matrimonial Procedure,* The Catholic University of America Canon Law Studies, Number 94, Washington, 1935.

Muniz, T., *Procedimientos Eclesiasticos,* 2 ed., 3 vols., Sevilla: Lib. de Sobrino de Isquierdo, 1926.

Noval, Josephus, *Commentarium Codicis Iuris Canonici,* IV, *De Processibus,* Pars I, *De Iudiciis,* Augustae Taurinorum: Marietti, 1920.

Panormitanus (Nicolaus de Tudeschis), *Commentaria in Quinque Libros Decretalium,* 8 vols., Venetiis, 1588.

Pirhing, Henricus, *Ius Canonicum in V. Libros Decretalium,* 5 vols., Dilingae, 1674-1678.

Reiffenstuel, Anacletus, *Ius Canonicum Universum,* 7 vols., Parisiis, 1864-1870.

Roberti, Franciscus, *De Processibus,* 2 vols., Romae: Apud Aedes Facultatis Iuridicae ad S. Apollinaris, 1926.

Rufinus, *Summa,* edited by Johann Friedrich von Schulte, Giessen: Verlag von Emil Roth, 1892.

Schmalzgrueber, Franciscus, *Ius Ecclesiasticum Universum,* 12 vols., Romae: Ex Typographia Rev. Cam. Apostolicae, 1844.

Tanquerey, Ad., *Synopsis Theologiae Moralis Et Pastoralis,* 7 ed., 3 vols., Romae: Desclee et Socii, 1922.

Thatcher-McNeal, *A Source Book for Medieval History,* New York: Charles Scribner's Sons, 1905.

Van Espen, Z., *Ius Ecclesiasticum Universum Ceteraque Scripta Omnia,* Venetiis, 1769.

Vermeersch, A.-Creusen, J., *Epitome Iuris Canonici cum Commentariis,* 3 ed., 3 vols., Romae, 1928.

Wanenmacher, Francis, *Canonical Evidence in Marriage Cases,* The Catholic University of America Canon Law Studies, Number 9, Washington, D. C., 1935.

Wenger, Leopold, *Institutionen Des Römischen Zivilprozessrechts,* München: Verlag der Hochschulbuchhandlung Max Hueber, 1925.

Wernz, Franciscus, *Ius Decretalium,* 6 vols., Romae, 1908-1913.

Wernz-Vidal, *Ius Canonicum ad Codicis Normam Exactum, Apud Aedes Universitatis Gregorianae,* 6 vols., Vol. VI, *De Processibus,* Romae, 1927.

Whalen, Donald, *The Value of Testimonial Evidence in Matrimonial Procedure,* The Catholic University of America Canon Law Studies, Number 99, Washington, 1935.

ALPHABETICAL INDEX

BIOGRAPHICAL NOTE

EUGENE J. MORIARTY was born on September 10, 1907, in St. Paul, Minnesota, and attended St. Mark's Parochial School of that city. He received his secondary education in St. Thomas Academy and Nazareth Hall Preparatory Seminary, St. Paul. His seminary course was made at the St. Paul Seminary. He was ordained to the Priesthood on June 4, 1932. In September, 1934, he enrolled in the School of Canon Law at the Catholic University of America from which he received the degrees of J.C.B. in 1935, and of J.C.L. in 1936.

CANON LAW STUDIES

1. Freriks, Rev. Celestine A., C.PP.S., J.C.D., Religious Congregations in Their External Relations, 121 pp., 1916.
2. Galliher, Rev. Daniel M., O.P., J.C.D., Canonical Elections, 117 pp., 1917.
3. Borkowski, Rev. Aurelius L., O.F.M., J.C.D., De Confraternitatibus Ecclesiasticis, 136 pp., 1918.
4. Castillo, Rev. Cayo, J.C.D., Disertacion Historico-Canonica sobre la Potestad del Cabildo en Sede Vacante o Impedida del Vicario Capitular, 99 pp., 1919 (1918).
5. Kubelbeck, Rev. William J., S.T.B., J.C.D., The Sacred Penitentiaria and Its Relation to Faculties of Ordinaries and Priests, 129 pp., 1918.
6. Petrovits, Rev. Joseph, J.C., S.T.D., J.C.D., The New Church Law on Matrimony, X-461 pp., 1919.
7. Hickey, Rev. John J., S.T.B., J.C.D., Irregularities and Simple Impediments in the New Code of Canon Law, 100 pp., 1920.
8. Klekotka, Rev. Peter J., S.T.B., J.C.D., Diocesan Consultors, 179 pp., 1920.
9. Wanenmacher, Rev. Francis, J.C.D., The Evidence in Ecclesiastical Procedure Affecting the Marriage Bond, 1920 (Printed 1935).
10. Golden, Rev. Henry Francis, J.C.D., Parochial Benefices in the New Code, IV-119 pp., 1921 (Printed 1925).
11. Koudelka, Rev. Charles J., J.C.D., Pastors, Their Rights and Duties According to the New Code of Canon Law, 211 pp., 1921.
12. Melo, Rev. Antonius, O.F.M., J.C.D., De Exemptione Regularium, X-188 pp., 1921.
13. Schaaf, Rev. Valentine Theodore, O.F.M., S.T.B., J.C.D., The Cloister, X-180 pp., 1921.
14. Burke, Rev. Thomas Joseph, S.T.D., J.C.D., Competence in Ecclesiastical Tribunals, IV-117 pp., 1922.
15. Leech, Rev. George Leo, J.C.D., A Comparative Study of the Constitution "Apostolicae Sedis" and the "Codex Juris Canonici," 179 pp., 1922.
16. Motry, Rev. Hubert Louis, S.T.D., J.C.D., Diocesan Faculties According to the Code of Canon Law, II-167 pp., 1922.
17. Murphy, Rev. George Lawrence, J.C.D., Delinquencies and Penalties in The Administration and the Reception of the Sacraments, IV-121 pp., 1923.
18. O'Reilly, Rev. John Anthony, S.T.B., J.C.D., Ecclesiastical Sepulture in the New Code of Canon Law, II-129 pp., 1923.
19. Michalicka, Rev. Wenceslas Cyrill, O.S.B., J.C.D., Judicial Procedure in Dismissal of Clerical Exempt Religious, 107 pp., 1923.

20. Dargin, Rev. Edward Vincent, S.T.B., J.C.D., Reserved Cases According to the Code of Canon Law, IV-103 pp., 1924.
21. Godfrey, Rev. John A., S.T.B., J.C.D., The Right of Patronage According to the Code of Canon Law, 153 pp., 1924.
22. Hagedorn, Rev. Francis Edward, J.C.D., General Legislation on Indulgences, II-154 pp., 1924.
23. King, Rev. James Ignatius, J.C.D., The Administration of the Sacraments to Dying Non-Catholics, V-141 pp., 1924.
24. Winslow, Rev. Francis Joseph, O.F.M., J.C.D., Vicars and Prefects Apostolic, IV-149 pp., 1924.
25. Correa, Rev. Jose Servelion, S.T.L., J.C.D., La Potestad Legislativa de la Iglesia Catolica, IV-127 pp., 1925.
26. Dugan, Rev. Henry Francis, A.M., J.C.D., The Judiciary Department of the Diocesan Curia, 87 pp., 1925.
27. Keller, Rev. Charles Frederick, S.T.B., J.C.D., Mass Stipends, 167 pp., 1925.
28. Paschang, Rev. John Linus, J.C.D., The Sacramentals According to the Code of Canon Law, 129 pp., 1925.
29. Pointek, Rev. Cyrillus, O.F.M., S.T.B., J.C.D., De Indulto Exclaustrationis necnon Saecularizationis, XIII-289 pp., 1925.
30. Kearney, Rev. Richard Joseph, S.T.B., J.C.D., Sponsors at Baptism According to the Code of Canon Law, IV-127 pp., 1925.
31. Bartlett, Rev. Chester Joseph, A.M., LL.B., J.C.D., The Tenure of Parochial Property in the United States of America, V-108 pp., 1926.
32. Kilker, Rev. Adrian Jerome, J.C.D., Extreme Unction, V-425 pp., 1926.
33. McCormick, Rev. Robert Emmett, J.C.D., Confessors of Religious, VIII-266 pp., 1926.
34. Miller, Rev. Newton Thomas, J.C.D., Founded Masses According to the Code of Canon Law, VII-93 pp., 1926.
35. Roelker, Rev. Edward G., S.T.D., J.C.D., Principles of Privilege According to the Code of Canon Law, XI-166 pp., 1926.
36. Bakalarczyk, Rev. Richardus, M.I.C., J.U.D., De Novitiatu, VIII-208 pp., 1927.
37. Pizzuti, Rev. Lawrence, O.F.M., J.U.L., De Parochis Religiosis, 1927. (Not Printed.)
38. Bliley, Rev. Nicholas Martin, O.S.B., J.C.D., Altars According to the Code of Canon Law, XIX-132 pp., 1927.
39. Brown, Mr. Brendan Francis, A.B., LL.M., J.U.D., The Canonical Juristic Personality with Special Reference to its Status in the United States of America, V-212 pp., 1927.
40. Cavanaugh, Rev. William Thomas, C.P., J.U.D., The Reservation of the Blessed Sacrament, VIII-101 pp., 1927.
41. Doheny, Rev. William J., C.S.C., A.B., J.U.D., Church Property: Modes of Acquisition, X-118 pp., 1927.
42. Feldhaus, Rev. Aloysius H., C.PP.S., J.C.D., Oratories, IX-141 pp., 1927.

43. KELLY, REV. JAMES PATRICK, A.B., J.C.D., The Jurisdiction of the Simple Confessor, X-208 pp., 1927.
44. NEUBERGER, REV. NICHOLAS J., J.C.D., Canon 6 or the Relation of the Codex Juris Canonici to the Preceding Legislation, V-95 pp. 1927.
45. O'KEEFE, REV. GERALD MICHAEL, J.C.D., Matrimonial Dispensations, Powers of Bishops, Priests, and Confessors, VIII-232 pp., 1927.
46. QUIGLEY, REV. JOSEPH A. M., A.B., J.C.D., Condemned Societies, 139 pp., 1927.
47. ZAPLOTNIK, REV. JOHANNES LEO, J.C.D., De Vicariis Foraneis, X-142 pp., 1927.
48. DUSKIE, REV. JOHN ALOYSIUS, A.B., J.C.D., The Canonical Status of the Orientals in the United States, VIII-196 pp., 1928.
49. HYLAND, REV. FRANCIS EDWARD, J.C.D., Excommunication, Its Nature, Historical Development and Effects, VIII-181 pp., 1928.
50. REINMANN, REV. GERALD JOSEPH, O.M.C., J.C.D., The Third Order Secular of Saint Francis, 201 pp., 1928.
51. SCHENK, REV. FRANCIS J., J.C.D., The Matrimonial Impediments of Mixed Religion and Disparity of Cult, XVI-318 pp., 1929.
52. COADY, REV. JOHN JOSEPH, S.T.D., J.U.D., A.M., The Appointment of Pastors, VIII-150 pp., 1929.
53. KAY, REV. THOMAS HENRY, J.C.D., Competence in Matrimonial Procedure, VIII-164 pp., 1929.
54. TURNER, REV. SIDNEY JOSEPH, C.P., J.U.D., The Vow of Poverty, XLIX-217 pp., 1929.
55. KEARNEY, REV. RAYMOND A., A.B., S.T.D., J.C.D., The Principles of Delegation, VII-149 pp., 1929.
56. CONRAN, REV. EDWARD JAMES, A.B., J.C.D., The Interdict, V-163 pp., 1930.
57. O'NEIL, REV. WILLIAM H., J.C.D., Papal Rescripts of Favor, VII-218 pp., 1930.
58. BASTNAGEL, REV. CLEMENT VINCENT, J.U.D., The Appointment of Parochial Adjutants and Assistants, XV-257 pp., 1930.
59. FERRY, REV. WILLIAM A., A.B., J.C.D., Stole Fees, V-136, pp., 1930.
60. COSTELLO, REV. JOHN MICHAEL, A.B., J.C.D., Domicile and Quasi-Domicile, VII-201 pp., 1930.
61. KREMER, REV. MICHAEL NICHOLAS, A.B., S.T.B., J.C.D., Church Support in the United States, VI-136 pp., 1930.
62. ANGULO, REV. LUIS, C.M., J.C.D., Legislation de la Iglesia sobre la intencion en la application de la Santa Misa, VII-104 pp., 1931.
63. FREY, REV. WOLFGANG, NORBERT, O.S.B., A.B., J.C.D., The Act of Religious Profession, VIII-174 pp., 1931.
64. ROBERTS, REV. JAMES BRENDAN, A.B., J.C.D., The Banns of Marriage, XIV-140 pp., 1931.
65. RYDER, REV. RAYMOND ALOYSIUS, A.B., J.C.D., Simony, IX-151 pp., 1931.

66. Campagna, Rev. Angelo, Ph.D., J.U.D., Il Vicario Generale del Vescovo, VII-205 pp., 1931.
67. Cox, Rev. Joseph Godfrey, A.B., J.C.D., The Administration of Seminaries, VI-124 pp., 1931.
68. Gregory, Rev. Donald J., J.U.D., The Pauline Privilege, XV-165 pp., 1931.
69. Donohue, Rev. John F., J.C.D., The Impediment of Crime, VII-110 pp., 1931.
70. Dooley, Rev. Eugene A., O.M.I., J.C.D., Church Law on Sacred Relics, IX-143 pp., 1931.
71. Orth, Rev. Clement Raymond, O.M.C., J.C.D., The Approbation of Religious Institutes, 171 pp., 1931.
72. Pernicone, Rev. Joseph M., A.B., J.C.D., The Ecclesiastical Prohibition of Books, XII-267 pp., 1932.
73. Clinton, Rev. Connell, A.B., J.C.D., The Paschal Precept, IX-108 pp., 1932.
74. Donnelly, Rev. Francis B., A.M., S.T.L., J.C.D., The Diocesan Synod, VIII-125 pp., 1932.
75. Torrente, Rev. Camilo, C.M.F., J.C.D., Las Processiones Sagradas, V-145 pp., 1932.
76. Murphy, Rev. Edwin J., C.PP.S., J.C.D., Suspension Ex Informata Conscientia, XI-122 pp., 1932.
77. Mackenzie, Rev. Eric F., A.M., S.T.L., J.C.D., The Delict of Heresy in its Commission, Penalization, Absolution, VII-124 pp., 1932.
78. Lyons, Rev. Avitus E., S.T.B., J.C.D., The Collegiate Tribunal of First Instance, XI-147 pp., 1932.
79. Connolly, Rev. Thomas A., J.C.D., Appeals, XI-195, pp., 1932.
80. Sangmeister, Rev. Joseph V., A.B., J.C.D., Force and Fear as Precluding Matrimonial Consent, V-211, pp., 1932.
81. Jaeger, Rev. Leo A., A.B., J.C.D., The Administration of Vacant and Quasi-Vacant Episcopal Sees in the United States, IX-229 pp., 1932.
82. Rimlinger, Rev. Herbert T., J.C.D., Error Invalidating Matrimonial Consent, VII-79 pp., 1932.
83. Barrett, Rev. John D. M., S.S., J.C.D., A Comparative Study of the Third Plenary Council of Baltimore and the Code, IX-221 pp., 1932.
84. Carberry, Rev. John J., Ph.D., S.T.D., J.C.D., The Juridical Form of Marriage, X-177 pp., 1934.
85. Dolan, Rev. John L., A.B., J.C.D., The Defensor Vinculi, XII, 157 pp., 1934.
86. Hannan, Rev. Jerome D., A.M., S.T.D., LL.B., J.C.D., The Canon Law of Wills, IX-517 pp., 1934.
87. Lemieux, Rev. Delisle A., A.M., J.C.D., The Sentence in Ecclesiastical Procedure, IX-131 pp., 1934.
88. O'Rourke, Rev. James J., A.B., J.C.D., Parish Registers, VII-109 pp., 1934.

89. TIMLIN, REV. BARTHOLOMEW, O.F.M., A.M., J.C.D., Conditional Matrimonial Consent, X-381 pp., 1934.
90. WAHL, REV. FRANCIS X., A.B., J.C.D., The Matrimonial Impediments of Consanguinity and Affinity, VI-125 pp., 1934.
91. WHITE, REV. ROBERT J., A.B., LL.B., S.T.B., J.C.D., Canonical Ante-Nuptial Promises and the Civil Law, VI-152 pp., 1934.
92. HERRERA, REV. ANTONIO PARRA, O.C.D., J.C.D., Legislacion Ecclesiastica sobra el Ayuno y la Abstinencia, XI-191 pp., 1935.
93. KENNEDY, REV. EDWIN J., J.C.D., The Special Matrimonial Process in Cases of Evident Nullity, X-165 pp., 1935.
94. MANNING, REV. JOHN J., A.B., J.C.D., Presumption of Law in Matrimonial Procedure, XI-111 pp., 1935.
95. MOEDER, REV. JOHN M., J.C.D., The Proper Bishop for Ordination and Dimissorial Letters, VII-135 pp., 1935.
96. O'MARA, REV. WILLIAM A., A.B., J.C.D., Canonical Causes for Matrimonial Dispensations, IX-155 pp., 1935.
97. REILLY, REV. PETER, J.C.D., Residence of Pastors, IX-81 pp., 1935.
98. SMITH, REV. MARINER T., O.P., S.T.Lr., J.C.D., The Penal Law for Religious, VII-169 pp., 1935.
99. WHALEN, REV. DONALD W., A.M., J.C.D., The Value of Testimonial Evidence in Matrimonial Procedure, XIII-297 pp., 1935.
100. CLEARY, REV. JOSEPH F., J.C.D., Canonical Limitations on the Alienation of Church Property, VIII-141 pp., 1936.
101. GLYNN, REV. JOHN C., J.C.D., The Promoter of Justice, XX-337 pp., 1936.
102. BRENNAN, REV. JAMES H., S.S., M.A., S.T.B., J.C.L., The Simple Convalidation of Marriage.
103. BRUNINI, REV. JOSEPH BERNARD, J.C.L., The Clerical Obligations of Canons 139 and 142.
104. CONNOR, REV. MAURICE, A.B., J.C.L., The Administrative Removal of Pastors.
105. GUILFOYLE, REV. MERLIN JOSEPH, J.C.L., Custom.
106. HUGHES, REV. JAMES AUSTIN, A.B., A.M., J.C.L., Witnesses in Criminal Trials of Clerics.
107. JANSEN, REV. RAYMOND J., A.B., S.T.L., J.C.L., Canonical Provisions for Catechetical Instruction.
108. KEALY, REV. JOHN JAMES, A.B., J.C.L., The Introductory Libellus in Church Court Procedure.
109. MCMANUS, REV. JAMES EDWARD, C.SS.R., J.C.L., The Administration of Temporal Goods in Religious Institutes.
110. MORIARITY, REV. EUGENE JAMES, J.C.L., Oaths in Ecclesiastical Courts.
111. RAINER, REV. ELIGIUS GEORGE, C.SS.R., J.C.L., Suspension of Clerics.
112. REILLY, REV. THOMAS F., C.SS.R., J.C.L., Visitation of Religious.

www.ingramcontent.com/pod-product-compliance
Lightning Source LLC
LaVergne TN
LVHW050204080826
844660LV00012B/349